# From Jim Crow to Jay-Z

## AFRICAN AMERICAN MUSIC IN GLOBAL PERSPECTIVE

Portia K. Maultsby and Mellonee V. Burnim, Series Editors

Archives of African American Music and Culture

Indiana University

*A list of books in the series appears at the end of this book.*

# FROM JIM CROW TO JAY-Z

## RACE, RAP, AND THE PERFORMANCE OF MASCULINITY

### BY MILES WHITE

UNIVERSITY OF ILLINOIS PRESS

*Urbana, Chicago, and Springfield*

Library of Congress Cataloging-in-Publication Data
White, Miles, 1954–
From Jim Crow to Jay-Z : race, rap, and the performance
of masculinity in American popular culture / Miles White.
p.   cm. — (African american music in global perspective)
Includes bibliographical references and index.
ISBN 978-0-252-03662-0 (cloth) — ISBN 978-0-252-07832-3 (pbk.)
1. Rap (Music)—Social aspects—United States.
2. African American men—Race identity.
3. Music and race. 4. Masculinity—United States.
I. Title.
ML3918.R37W53       2011
305.38'896073—dc22       2011016143

*For my mother, Mary White Mason, for persevering;*
*And to Nazgul Koshoeva and Erica Carlino, for Prague.*

# Contents

# Acknowledgments

The journalist Wallace Terry once commented that every book is born in debt, and this book is no different. There are many people who have contributed in some way or another to its existence. It began as a dissertation at the University of Washington and is first indebted to the faculty of the ethnomusicology department for the teaching assistantships that got me through graduate school. My thanks also to Dr. Johnnella Butler, the UW Office of Minority Affairs, and the Bank of America for providing a much needed dissertation year writing fellowship where early ideas began to take shape.

The manuscript was substantially revised during a two-year residency as a Riley Scholar-in-Residence at the Colorado College in Colorado Springs. I would like to thank the school and especially Dean Victor Nelson-Cisneros for his unwavering support over the years. A special thanks and acknowledgment for the inspiration of scholars Portia Maultsby, Mellonee Burnim, Adrienne Seward, Cheryl Keyes, Deborah Wong, and Eileen Hayes, who have all offered encouragement over the years. A thanks to Dr. John Stewart for directing me to the work of Robert Plant Armstrong. A warm acknowledgment to Dan Shanahan and Juraj Hvorecky, brilliant scholars, good friends, brothers in arms; and to Eva Farady, for compiling the index, doing hours of proofreading, and for her selfless devotion to my well being. A final thanks to Joan Catapano, Jennifer Clark, Daniel Nasset, Matthew Smith, Kathleen Kornell, Maria denBoer, and others at the University of Illinois Press who took the book upon their shoulders and saw it through.

# Introduction

In *Playing in the Dark*, Toni Morrison offers a compelling reading of the American literary canon that exposes a largely unremarked but salient "Africanist presence" embedded within the nation's great works of literature. Morrison interrogates the assumption that the American literary canon has not been substantially influenced by four hundred years of the African and African American presence in the United States. In so doing she introduces a refreshing reading of the national literature that allows for a richer and more profound understanding of the American character, one that cannot be separated from its multiracial heritage through what she deems "the process of organizing American coherence through a distancing Africanism,"[1] a project that continues unabated to the present day.

Morrison's criticism offers an opportunity to reconsider how African American music and questions around race have also helped to construct our national character and culture. If the contemplation of a peripheral black presence is critical to our understanding of American literature, then we are compelled to ask similar questions about our popular music. It is not just that African American sacred and secular music has served as the critical foundation for American popular music, but that American culture itself would be impossible to imagine without the black presence ever-residing at its margins, occasionally pushing its way into the mainstream and transforming it palpably and profoundly. This book draws a broad arc between the earliest form of popular music, one that is only marginally related to but nonetheless derived from black cultural expressions—American minstrelsy—and one of the most recent forms of popular music—contemporary hip-hop and the cultural milieu that surrounds it. It examines a number of themes related to performance and the black male body, representations of black masculinity, the construction of emotional affect or feeling around these, and the uses and misuses of black male subjectivity that have helped to shape perceptions and attitudes regarding black males in the American racial imagination. While acknowledging that the popular and scholarly historiography of hip-hop culture has yet not adequately addressed the role of women in that history, this is unabashedly a book about men and masculinities, although it is indebted to many feminist scholars who have expanded our understanding of gender and performance.

While it is also the case that women's studies and gender studies began largely as a way to include women's excluded histories, gender studies cannot or should not preclude the study of men if only to interrogate presumptions of male privilege and the kinds of constructions of masculinity that I critique. I make a number of connections between masculinity and race as kinds of ritualized performance that have particular types of aesthetic markers and that depend upon certain histories and cultural memories. Writing about masculinity arguably favors a gender position already privileged in many ways, but my intent is to interrogate masculinity as well as racial performance—of blackness *and* of whiteness—in the context of one of the most commercially and culturally important musical styles of the last quarter century, one that has arguably privileged the male body and performance more than any popular musical form since minstrelsy, and minstrelsy itself, the most important popular musical form in American history since it was the first. I bookend minstrelsy and hardcore hip-hop because they privilege the performance of both masculinity and race and because through them black and white males alike have used essentially the same set of signifiers to construct models of self and identity for themselves. I would argue that performances of race and masculinity have produced social consequences that extend far beyond the spectacle presented on stage. Obviously, issues of appropriation and authenticity become salient as does the fact we are dealing with different historical and cultural spaces. Nonetheless, these two forms of music and performance continue to have great relevance and resonance in discussing race, masculinity, and the ways in which the poetics of the body contributes to their respective musical practices.

In many ways, hip-hop music and culture have brought issues of gender to the forefront, but scholarly studies have failed to fully investigate all the ways in which hardcore styles of hip-hop in particular have recast ideas about masculinity and the performance of the body. There has been no paucity of writings that have tended to focus on the ways in which hardcore rap and many black males who participate in it have perpetuated misogyny, but another part of this discussion should engage how hardcore music and culture have helped to (re)construct and (re)define notions of masculinity and ideals of male performance in which misogynistic and homophobic attitudes are encouraged through the rejection of the feminine. What many books on contemporary black popular music and culture, including hardcore hip-hop, have also not fully addressed is how the most pejorative representations of black masculinity engaged as performance in global popular media perpetuate negative feelings and racial attitudes that demonize young black males. This has occurred in both the United States and other countries where African American culture—if the richness and complexity of this idea is apprehended at all in other parts of the world, and there is much evidence to suggest that it is not—is reduced to gold chains, expectations of violence and criminal activity, notions of deviance, and 'hood tales.[2]

This book begins, then, with a discussion around race, masculinity, and their performance in the context of popular music and its beginnings in minstrelsy on the one end, and moves at the other, to the ways in which contemporary hard/hardcore styles of hip-hop performance and the culture of masculinity that surrounds it have reformulated and helped to articulate new models of self and identity for many young males over the last quarter century. It examines in particular the ways in which objectified, fetishized, and commodified representations of black males and the projections of masculinity associated with them have been adopted and co-opted as performative tropes, ones that recur at different places at different times using the same language of codes, signs, and gestures that have exerted a defining influence on young male constructions of identity. I problematize the gender constructions of post–new school (marked by the arrival of Run-DMC in 1983) expressions of masculinity in hip-hop to suggest that they are not *naturalized* any more than any gender performance is somehow natural in itself, but that they are derived from a certain cultural and musical context that reifies historical representations of black males through various modes of performance practices that play upon the body.

Minstrelsy profoundly affected the ways in which black males were later represented in popular culture, the real and systemic consequences of which linger in the American racial imagination up to the present day, particularly in hardcore hip-hop performance, which reinscribes the black male as brute or the folkloric bad nigger figure, a lawless man feared by blacks and whites alike and whom I discuss in detail in the pages to come. The performance of whiteness in hardcore hip-hop, on the other hand, reconfigures the masquerade of racial performance but nonetheless retains notions of deviant black male subjectivity as its most defining subtext. I consequently return on several occasions to another recurring trope in American culture, that of the white Negro, given perhaps its most graphic explication by Norman Mailer in his 1957 essay "The White Negro: Superficial Reflections on the Hipster," a paean to the pleasures of *opting out* of whiteness and *acting out* behind the mask of blackness. The white Negro actually makes his debut in popular culture (in fact, *creating* popular culture) with T. D. Rice's minstrel character Jim Crow in the early 1800s and has appeared in any number of guises since. The white Negro and the bad nigger are both iconic figures that have appeared in American popular culture—in literature, in films, on stage and television, and in popular music—with some consistency since the early nineteenth century. They represent America's now centuries-old carnivalesque of racial masquerade that has been central to the formation of masculinity and working-class identity and that reached an apotheosis with hip-hop culture and hardcore rap music beginning in the 1980s.

Mailer's caricature of the white Negro, writes historian and literary critic Louis Menand, "is built up from the proposition that American Negroes by virtue of their alienation from mainstream American society, are natural existentialists who not only have better orgasms but who also appreciate the cathartic effects of physical violence."[3] The aim of the white Negro and hipster has always been the imitation of the bad nigger in order to, as Mailer writes, be "with it." What this has ultimately evolved into is a politics of racialized masculine desire in which it is no longer desirable to merely be *with it* but *to be it*, so that it is no longer necessarily the case, as Menand suggests, that "the sort of gender roles central to Mailer's imagination have disappeared from the repertoire of contemporary identity."[4] The mainstreaming of hip-hop culture and the idea of the hard man—a revisitation of the black brute who is immune to physical and emotional pain—have had a transfiguring effect on contemporary constructions of masculine performance over the last twenty-five or so years for males of all racial and ethnic groups. If Mailer's writing seems to enact a panic about masculinity and its fate, as Menand suggests, then he might well be pleased with the way things have turned out, since white Negroism has become de rigueur for the performance of maleness among legions of adolescents in post–hip-hop America, and the bad nigger has become its most defining trope.

My use of the literary term *trope* in this context is also meant to suggest how representation may be seen as a kind of figurative language, as a figure of thought as opposed to a figure of speech, one that recontextualizes a literal reference into a figurative one. What I am suggesting here is that visual representation and the use of visual images are often metaphorical, and that over the history of American culture representation has been used to construct a language of discourse where the black male as subject(ivity) and the black male body have become primary vehicles and sites for fears as well as fantasies of the racial Other. These recurring tropes remain largely implicit yet always implied in popular music and media, including film, computer games, television (evening news programs in urban markets remain particularly pernicious in this regard), magazine advertisements, and newspapers. As the line between the metaphorical and the real becomes increasingly blurred in post-1960s hip-hop America, we should perhaps interrogate how popular music has helped to instigate and perpetuate a metaphorical language around representation and blackness in the American racial imagination. What are the lingering historical and contemporary implications of these implied constructions of race for black men and black people generally? What are the implications of a racial masquerade in which other kinds of bodies appropriate and perform interpretations of blackness and black male subjectivity, and what are we to read from such performances? With respect to hardcore styles of rap, how do such performances inculcate attitudes and perceptions about black men and black masculinity? How do Vanilla Ice and Eminem figure into all of this?

While the fact of racial masquerade is itself not new, the confluence of race (particularly its primary bifurcations of blackness and whiteness), masculinity, and performance as a focus for scholarly inquiry seems to be relatively recent, coming into focus in the 1980s and 1990s as hardcore rap moved from the periphery of popular culture to its center and that resulted in a virtual renaissance of new scholarly work around race in American popular culture across disciplines largely related to cultural studies.[5] What I address in a sustained way are ideas around affective emotional response and the ways that kinds of performance—of race, gender, the body—become instantiated in the process of certain types of musical performance and in fact *are* part of the performance. I am concerned with the ways the black male body has been objectified through heightened modes of speech and behavior and (re)circulated in popular culture, where "little restraint has been attached to its uses."[6] The fetishism of the black male as the new antiheroic social outlaw in hardcore hip-hop is suggestive of how representations of the black male body have been both colonized for pleasure and financial gain while simultaneously enabling the rhetorical move that recodes crime as blackness.

Ronald Radano and Philip Bohlman posit the term *the racial imagination* to suggest the "shifting matrix of ideological constructions of difference associated with body type and color" that help to critically construct individual and group identity in the current historical moment.[7] The imagination of race, these authors further contend, "not only informs perceptions of musical practice but is at once constituted within and projected into the social through sound."[8] It is quite logical, then, to make critical links between the body, musical sound, and the construction of identity that are relevant to a serious appraisal of the ways in which popular music performance helps to shape ideas around masculinity and race in general and blackness and maleness in particular. Scholars such as Judith Butler, Linda Tucker, Tricia Rose, Eric Lott, bell hooks, Murray Foreman, Deborah Wong, Ingrid Monson, Cheryl Keyes, Simon Frith, Mark Anthony Neal, Greg Dimitriadis, Tony Jefferson, and David Roediger have been critical to my own understanding and thinking about the intersections between race and gender and negotiations around blackness, whiteness, and the construction of identity for young males in American culture. These authors have brought to the subject the complexity and intellectual depth it deserves and the interdisciplinary breadth it requires. Nonetheless, the body of scholarship that looks at race as an informing subtext of masculinity studies is inexplicably modest, particularly since black males and contestations around authenticity and masculinity have been extraordinarily privileged in popular culture and mass media over the last quarter century.

The study of hip-hop music and culture continues to have profound implications for understanding how race is constructed and negotiated in popular culture. Tricia Rose observed more than a decade ago that the themes, ideas, and contradictions of the music in its myriad of styles are some of "the most disturbing, powerful, and important to have emerged from any cultural workers in quite some time,"[9] and this continues to be the case even though many scholars working in the academy, particularly those engaged in the teaching of African American music, continue to see race and the contingencies around blackness and whiteness in American culture as unproblematic. Nonetheless, the contradictions around race, performance, appropriation, and representation deserve to be interrogated and their most egregious facets critiqued by those of us who study and support the music and culture of hip-hop, and this book is my attempt to do so. In Chapter one, I examine minstrel performance as the first construction of an *absent black presence* in American popular music, signified by the minstrel mask, and as the first sustained project involving the fetishization and commodification of black male subjectivity. Chapter two focuses on comparisons between minstrelsy and constructions of black masculinity in hip-hop music and culture, particularly the context of hard and hardcore styles of rap performance. Chapter three looks at the ways in which the body, aesthetic features of hip-hop music, and the material culture that surrounds it are deployed to construct affect and help delineate between what is meant by hard and hardcore, both as music and as masculine performance. It also traces the historical evolution of hip-hop culture from a largely benign music to something more malevolent. Chapter four discusses the performance of blackness and masculinity in hip-hop performance, the trope of the bad nigger and the notion of the hard man and how African American performers have engaged the sign of blackness in both pejorative and empowering ways. It also discusses the crack cocaine epidemic in the 1980s and how the intrusion of gang and drug cultures contributed to the transformation of hip-hop culture, the performance of masculinity within that culture, and the influence of a number of seminal artists including Run-DMC, N.W.A, Public Enemy, and Jay-Z. Chapter five discusses whiteness, masculine desire, and the animating absent black presence now inverted since its inception in minstrelsy. It also looks at a number of successful white performers of black music styles, including Elvis Presley, Vanilla Ice, Eminem, and Brother Ali, and addresses whether there are more or less ethical ways in which white and other youth may engage hip-hop culture and appropriations of black male subjectivity.

Some of the chapter titles (and various subheadings as well) reflect some playful riffing, the jazzman's most profound gesture of respect to the ideas of another, which borrow from or signify on works associated with well-known authors, including Ralph Ellison (Shadow and Act), James Baldwin (The Fire Next Time), and Robin D. G. Kelley (Race Rebels), writers whom I look up to as mentors and giants.

# 1. Shadow and Act
## American Popular Music and the Absent Black Presence

The body was an indispensable component of musical performance until the arrival of sound recording in the early part of the twentieth century. In essence, the representation of live music as sound object, stored on prefabricated discs and mechanically reproduced on phonographs, meant that the social enjoyment of music no longer required a physical body in the room playing an instrument or singing a song. The dissemination of new songs in the popular music industry gradually segued away from sheet music into the new medium of phonograph recordings and later into radio. As these gradually penetrated both upper- and middle-class urban homes and later working-class homes as well, two things in particular became increasingly true. The first is that these technologies dramatically transformed the way that vernacular styles of music were consumed in rural communities, while also allowing music produced by the few to be shared by the many; phonograph records meant music was able to be broadly disseminated and enjoyed outside socially or racially segregated communities. The second thing is that technology would set the circumstances that made possible a distancing of black music from its socio-cultural origins in a way that would allow it to be claimed as cultural property by others, something that had rarely happened in the social history of American music.

In effect, the advent of recorded sound allowed for the presence of black people and black bodies to become dispensable in the consumption of styles of music with which they were intimately associated, and whose primary creative impulses came from black aesthetic practices. This became pointedly the case with early recordings of jazz, the first major music genre to emerge in the age of popular recording. The Original Dixieland Jazz Band, a group of white musicians who recorded their first sides in New York City in 1917, claimed authorship of the music when many people outside New Orleans had never heard of it. It is true that these musicians helped to open the commercial market for the music, but like later white musicians who adopted jazz and other black styles of music and made them available to a broader audience, a tension was nonetheless created between embracing an invigorating Africanist presence and the simultaneous need to erase it, between a desire to retain the broad outlines of a uniquely characteristic cultural production but deny its deep rootedness in the culture of African Americans. The historical love of black music by whites in the United States has always been troubled by the fact of blackness itself, by "the trauma provoked by the introduction of the black body into white space."[1] In the century before jazz's rise to prominence, minstrelsy performance practice and the reproduction of caricatures of black people on the covers of sheet music represented perhaps the first example of this ambivalence in popular music in that it erased, appropriated, and (re)presented a kind of faux black subjectivity for mainstream consumption. Neither the white minstrel in blackface nor white minstrel songs of the day offered authentic renderings of black music or black culture, but rather signified upon black subjectivities as absent presences. Owing to the dominance of minstrel and coon songs in popular music in the latter decades of the nineteenth century and the early years of the twentieth, these kinds of representations of African Americans in popular culture became suddenly ubiquitous, a startling phenomenon given the estranged status of black people in the broader society. Physical representation of black bodies in popular music in the late 1800s to the early 1920s arguably begins the cultural policing of black bodies through the gaze of whiteness, which would be critical to the erection of post-Reconstruction black codes and Jim Crow laws that erased or severely restricted the presence of black bodies in white space.

Minstrelsy practice required a body at the level of performance, but not a black one; rather, it called for the representation of blackness constructed in the white American racial imagination of the time. After the Civil War, black male performers who began to access the entertainment industry in minstrel troupes, and they did so in large numbers, were required to do so in blackface since the black mask conformed to by now deeply embedded social stereotypes of black masculine subjectivity. Sheet music, which also required only faux black bodies, displayed grotesque caricatures of black people that were intended to provoke any range of affective responses, none of them generous and some clearly malicious as the Civil War approached and the prospect of thousands of freed black slaves became palpable. Images such as T. D. Rice's countrified southern character Jim Crow or the buffoonish northern dandy used for the cover of George Washington Dixon's composition *Zip Coon*[2] were nonetheless fairly benign compared to the vile images deployed on covers of much sheet music which had appeared by mid-century. A particularly egregious example was the cover for coon shouter May Irvin's Broadway hit "The Bully Song," performed in 1895 for *The Widow Jones*, and which depicts a black male figure that can only be described as bestial, garishly dressed in ill-fitting clothing with huge red lips, hairy oversized hands, and wildly crazed eyes. The unsettling effect of the caricature was finished off by an open straight razor in his right hand. The depiction is made powerful by the aggregation of its parts, and suggests the particularly vicious nature of racial representation of blacks prior to and for decades following Reconstruction, as black claims to socio-economic and political enfranchisement increased. Such images of black people transfigured through the ideological racial imaginings of whites into absurd caricatures would create an enormous complex of products from soap to pancake mix and contribute to a culture of "commodity racism"[3] that has been as integral to the development of representational practices in popular culture as black music has been to the formation of popular music practices. The uses of black male bodies in particular suggest the ways in which "white America has made an art of manipulating the images of black men to suit social, political, and economic agendas that share the goal of containing African American men."[4]

Ralph Ellison, in his 1958 article "Change the Joke and Slip the Yoke," suggests that the minstrel mask represented perhaps the first commodified racial fetish that was uniquely American, "an inseparable part of the national iconography" but one in which "the Negro is reduced to a negative sign that usually appears in a comedy of the grotesque and the unacceptable."[5] As commodity, obvious parallels can be made between the practices and iconographies of minstrelsy and the slave trade, where one deals quite literally in the trading of black flesh and the other deals in the figurative trade of representations of blackness, although both involve a usurpation of agency of the black body. Similar ideological assumptions belie both practices, and both were critical in building a national character that drew on the exchange value of the objectified black body. The minstrel mask signifies the donning of blackness as its primary trope, but it also signifies the larger trope of the racial or ethnic Other. From the protective and surrogate mask of an emasculated black image, white males became the clowning, winking instigators of all manner of cultural mayhem. In his 1995 history of blackface minstrelsy, *Love and Theft*, a recuperative study that has broadened and legitimated the discussion of minstrelsy and its place in American popular culture, Eric Lott suggests that minstrelsy was more than merely a racist art form conceived to humiliate African Americans, but was also a way for white performers to comment on the events and times in which they lived, although this certainly included ambivalence about the black presence in their midst. The minstrel mask allowed multiple social critiques to issue forth and was a space that invited multiple interpretations of the genre itself—its ideological scope, the ambitions of its performers, and the pleasures paid for and enjoyed by its audiences.

In the early nineteenth century, blackface performance was often an especially defiant gesture by disempowered young white workers, who in abstracting themselves as blacks created an oppositional strategy to existing structures of power and social conservatism. Although masking offered a way to play with collective fears of an alienating black Other, it also complicated whiteness since ethnic Italians, Germans, Irish, Jews, and those in positions of power and class privilege were often lambasted in blackface performance, even though some of these, particularly Irish and later Jewish males, proliferated and profited from the blackface art. The minstrel show "was the first among many later manifestations, nearly always allied with images of black culture, which allowed youths to resist merchant-defined external impostures and to express a distinctive style."[6]

The minstrel mask allowed these youth to engage in acts that were interpretively fluid and politically expedient, opening a space in which to alternately flirt with desire and repulsion while avoiding retribution from the racial masquerade by employing a Janus-faced camouflage. On the one hand, they signaled to congenial audiences their mutual identification with blackness and a sense of social alienation, while, on the other, when performing before hostile audiences, they disavowed and belittled their subject. In this way the pleasures of racial transgression were instantly accessible but immune to social repercussion. The mask easily cavorted between sympathetic identification and fear, a delicate play of the racial carnivalesque that worked for more than one hundred years to "safely facilitate an exchange of energies between two otherwise rigidly bounded and policed cultures,"[7]and that would critically factor into the formation of a self-consciously white working-class identity. It is no less true, however, that blackface performance by whites was done at the expense of blacks and not necessarily to their benefit until around the mid-1800s and particularly following the Civil War, when blackface troupes featuring African American performers were in vogue. African American minstrelsy nurtured the first generation of black entertainers and formed the bedrock of virtually all subsequent African American stage and theatrical performance—from vaudeville and musicals to stand-up comedy and film.

It is likewise true that black minstrel performance did not provide the strategic counterbalance to the pejorative representations of white minstrelsy that some had hoped. The historical impact and consequence of white performances of blackface and the negative stereotyping of black people it perpetuated somehow became more indelibly etched into the American racial imagination than the work of black performers who tried to insert more authenticity and humanity into the art form and "break down the ill feeling that existed toward the colored people."[8] One reason for that certainly is that white minstrelsy, despite the space for oppositional subversion that it opened up, nonetheless became a space where the fears, resentments, hostilities, and imagined threats of emancipated blacks were played out. The trajectory of black and white minstrel performance would follow largely segregated paths after the war owing to a number of unsettled issues such as black social advancement and the trauma provoked by the presence of the black body in white space. Even after the arrival of vaudeville and the diversification of stage material that it made possible, the most egregious aspects of white minstrelsy found other forms of expression in books, stage musicals, and film. Another reason for the evolutionary racial bifurcation of American popular culture has certainly been that whites have often felt more comfortable consuming black cultural expressions when they came from other white performers. This truth has borne itself out in the historical segregation of the performance arts in America for most of the twentieth century, where separate black and white traditions have formed in virtually every area of entertainment, from vaudeville and musicals to film and popular music, represented by white performers from the Original Dixieland Jazz Band and Benny Goodman to Elvis Presley and Eminem. Black performers prospered regardless and formed a community of highly talented artists for whom other blacks became their natural audience, and this remains largely the case notwithstanding a good deal of racial border crossings and cultural borrowings from both sides. Nonetheless, it may have been wishful thinking to presume that the popularity of post–Civil War minstrelsy, the success of emergent vaudeville traditions, and black performers as acclaimed as Bert Williams and George Walker would form the basis, if not for racial healing and cultural understanding between blacks and whites, then of intervention "to subvert or amend the message of minstrelsy by substituting a new messenger."[9] The history of race relations in the postwar period and through much of the next century suggests that this has largely not been the case. Rather, the deleterious representations of blacks produced by white minstrelsy became deeply ingrained in the American psyche, such that the "momentum of over 150 years of derogatory images and characterizations [in popular culture] flowed down on our heads with real consequence because white power enforced and depended on black racial identity."[10]

It seems somewhat incongruous, then, that the white minstrel and his working-class audiences should identify with blacks as outsiders and transform black performance into a vocabulary of social commentary that helps to begin a tradition of white working-class counterinsurgency and subversion expressed through popular music. Minstrelsy did indeed establish a popular theater responding to the codes, parlance, and sensibilities of working-class whites while it lampooned wealthy bluenoses, but it also set the stage for the visual representation of African Americans throughout the remainder of the nineteenth century, where "images of blacks in artworks most often iterated limited or derogatory perceptions held by most whites and helped create a visual iconography for black representation."[11] These representations helped to naturalize a social order in which blacks were marginalized and helped to shape white perceptions around blackness for more than a generation. Minstrelsy represents the first sustained cultural project in which the agency of the black male body and black subjectivity are usurped by white actors as fetishized commodity. The effects of this particular racial counterfeit have been critical in the construction of black masculinity in the white imagination up to the present day.

Popular culture and mass media in particular, including film, television, video, and music, have been among "the most fertile social arenas in which African Americans engaged each other (and whites) over questions of African American presence in the United States."[12] The representations that have been generated through such media have generally been pejorative even as they have put the sign of blackness and the debates surrounding it at the center of a much broader discourse around race in American culture. The struggle over representation, over blackness as sign and signifier in popular music, arguably became most critical following minstrelsy and in the early years of the twentieth century with ragtime and jazz, which would ultimately exert an immeasurable influence not only on Western music but also on the broad concept of Western art as well. Arthur Jafa identifies the appropriation of African art in the development of European modernism and the creation of jazz in the United States as the two defining moments of radical black aesthetic intervention and subversion in Western art. In these critical interventions, the encounter between Africanism and blackness is "appropriated for the associative value [it lends] to modernism—to being hip, sophisticated, ultra-urbane."[13] Pablo Picasso's use of distortion in his cubist works, for instance, suggests the existential fragmentation and cultural alienation of the black body in white space, a distortion that borders on the grotesque and recalls the imagery employed in sheet music of coon songs, plantation songs, and minstrel songs and in blackface performance itself.

Nonetheless, the appropriation of the black body as the grotesque Other may be seen as a contradictory impulse of attraction and repulsion that on the one hand advanced cultural modernism in artistic movements but that on the other hand marked the black body in white space as always discordant, incongruous, and decontexualized.

Jazz musical and cultural practices ruptured centuries-old melodic, harmonic, and rhythmic conventions of Western art music and pointed to a new way of being in the world as a result of the manifest being of its creators: the way they spoke and behaved, the way they dressed, their idiomatic manner of occupying (and penetrating) space, their individual styles and philosophies, and the consensual articulations of the aesthetic and generative processes of the music. The black body in the culture of jazz became the object of deviancy and thus fetishism because it stood outside mainstream cultural values and Victorian ideals of social conformity, creating a sense of freedom and an allure for the exotic as well as a disconcerting anxiety certainly duplicated in the jagged rhythms and discordant timbres of the music. These two instances of cultural insurgency are difficult to quantify because their implications are so enormous. They also problematize the black body in the Western imagination since it "functions, in the Western mind-set, as the sign of a radically different ontology, which of course threatened the Eurocentric belief in itself as the defining model of humanity."[14] White America has had to balance the tension between seeing itself from an ideologically superior position in the history of humanity and yet fetishizing a deep desire for an exotic Other that existed outside itself. This conundrum has often been resolved by what feminist critic bell hooks has characterized as "eating the Other,"[15] the appropriation and consumption of the object of racial desire by whites so that what blackness purports to represent is seen through and interpreted by them. Black bodies are subsequently simply erased or merely controlled through racial transvesting.

In *Body and Soul: The Making of American Modernism*, Robert Crunden also locates jazz as a dominant factor in the formation of modernist ideas in the arts after the turn of the twentieth century, suggesting some found in it "a refreshing primitivism, a liberating search for new forms, a beguiling openness to the validity of emotional expression"[16]—all things that helped to define it as something particularly and uniquely American in a country where what passed as high culture still largely looked to Europe. The primitivism and validity of emotional expression that jazz introduced into American bourgeois conservatism and that later inspired the bohemianism of the 1950s white hipster—avant-garde "beat culture" intellectual writers including Allen Ginsberg and Jack Kerouac and jazz musicians such as Gerry Mulligan, Lee

Tristano, Lee Konitz, Dave Brubeck, and Chet Baker—have been as liberating as those same expressions that blackface minstrelsy allowed. Jazz in the twentieth century was as critically implicated in the construction of popular culture and in ways of viewing race in American culture as was minstrelsy in the nineteenth century. The American modernists and artisans who gravitated toward jazz or adopted its edgy aesthetic energy and social milieu "felt themselves to be alienated outsiders, even when skin color or economic circumstances might indicate otherwise."[17] This dynamic would reappear with white teens who embraced African American rhythm and blues after World War II and hip-hop at the end of the twentieth century.

We may not be far enough away from the present moment to assess the historical impact of hip-hop music on American culture at the turn of the twenty-first century, but performance practices identified with African American cultural expressions that circulate in hip-hop culture are critically implicated in the formation of any notion of a postmodernist aesthetic in American popular culture nearly a century after the nascent modernism of the early 1900s. Crunden speaks of "the interdisciplinary quality of American modernism"[18] that finds expression across a spectrum of aesthetic enterprises, and demonstrates how the rise of jazz from 1917 forward is deeply implicated in the aesthetic innovations of the period of high modernism in 1920s and 1930s following World War I. This appears no less true in terms of a postmodernist (a contradictory term after all since modernism is never truly in a historical *after*, but always occurs in the present as a dynamic, organic, and ongoing process of cultural change and reevaluation), postindustrial (a more tangible term given the very real decline of American manufacturing and the industrial infrastructure that supported blue-collar, working-class families) American popular culture where hip-hop music and culture have provided a new set of aesthetic practices that construct a decentered, fragmented text through strategies involving pastiche, parody, montage, irony, space/time distortion, self-reflexivity, and a blurring of distinctions between highbrow and lowbrow. These aesthetic strategies redefine that particular moment of American modernism from the early twentieth century and privilege new cultural sensibilities and technologies of communication. In many ways, the jazz era and the hip-hop nation could not be more profoundly different in terms of musical aesthetics and the technologies of reproduction, but there are continuities as well as ruptures that may be found in the ways that popular culture and whiteness have been constructed, negotiated, and represented around the organizing tropes of blackness and black music. This evolutionary process cannot be divorced from the progression of historical events and contestations for social justice and representational dignity that became foregrounded during the era of American minstrelsy. In *Images of the Outsider in American Law and Culture*, Richard Delgado and Jean Stefancic discuss how the first appearance of the "comic Negro" Sambo figure in the 1781 stage play *The Divorce* assuaged fears about the black male Other. White performers in blackface portrayed the buffoon so that consequently "the black man's potential as a sexual and economic competitor was minimized by portraying him as an object of laughter."[19] African American blackface performers, even those as eloquent and cultured as Williams, would not escape playing the fool even after minstrelsy began its decline as the popular entertainment of the day.

Trumpeter Louis Armstrong, who more than any other musical figure of his time began to define modernism in jazz, would never get past this fawning sop to the wealthy patrons he entertained. Although Duke Ellington would begin to move toward a more serious-minded approach to black musical representation in his extended spirituals and conceptual works, it would be bebop performers of the late 1950s and free jazz artists in the 1960s who started to construct new representational models for performers of black music as these styles themselves adopted new musical languages using angular rhythmic structures, harmonic dissonance, and a range of vernacular idiomatic sounds meant to reflect black cultural resistance to Eurocentric forms of hegemonic containment. Many of these musicians criticized Armstrong's obsequious stage demeanor and offered nothing of themselves that could not be discovered in the music they played, which they considered sufficient enough. Charlie Parker and Miles Davis were among the first bebop musicians who rarely offered ingratiating smiles to audiences or attempted to appear gracious. Davis in particular was castigated for his apparent aloofness, which was nothing more than a refusal to surrender his dignity for the privilege of presenting his music. In so doing, he alternatively became an object of white fascination and resentment.[20]

The post-swing generation of jazz musicians that included Parker, Davis, Ornette Coleman, Archie Shepp, John Coltrane, Albert Ayler, Charles Mingus, Cecil Taylor, Anthony Braxton, and others presented themselves in ways that were as defiant and uncompromising as the music they were creating. Jazz musicians of these eras redefined both the performance and the performer in gestures that challenged socially accepted norms around music, masculinity, and blackness and can be easily seen as a kind of middle ground from minstrelsy to the current historical moment. Comparisons can certainly be drawn between the militant strategies adopted by this generation of jazz musicians to the ways hip-hop artists have recast music and masculine performance since the early 1980s, so that there may not be such a great distance to transverse after all between the *keeping it real* and the *trying to make it real compared to what.* Facial expression, physical comportment, and emotional coldness in hardcore rap performance of masculinity may be seen as survival strategies for black males negotiating the capricious realities of inner-city life, but they also embrace an uncompromising projection of blackness and masculinity that, like discordant sounds, offensive rhetoric, and profane language, reject mainstream norms of the socially acceptable.

Like 1960s jazz and other expressive forms that gave voice to the black arts movement of the time, hardcore rap performance has (re)framed black masculinity within a socio-cultural context where the public expressions of anger and rage are privileged affective strategies, even though they are largely depoliticized. The act of mean mugging in the performance of the hard masculine ideal in contemporary hip-hop adopts a privileged subjectivity that has historically been reserved for white males, a posture of confident masculinity in which one must project powerful emotions if one is to gain respect. If minstrelsy was a performance practice in which masculine power was denied to black males, hardcore rap performance represents an opposite extreme, where black masculinity is recuperated in an arena of affective representation and performance of the body—through speech, music, language, sartorial display, and gesture—that is certainly not without its excesses, as we will see. What hip-hop culture has done in the age of video culture is to reintroduce the black male body (with a vengeance would not be much of an overstatement) into a field of play in American popular culture that makes it even more available for the usurpation of agency by others. What this has allowed in turn, is a reinscription of aspects of minstrelsy practice—white bodies imitating black bodies but through any number of alternative affective gestures that do not employ the burnt cork—that are circulated into a global culture of visual imagery where they are again appropriated as public property. Hip-hop brings minstrelsy full circle, with the troubling difference that the carnivalesque of the grotesque implied in its racial play now comes not from outside black American culture, but from within it.

## 2. The Fire This Time

### Black Masculinity and the Politics of Racial Performance

The transatlantic slave trade and chattel slavery in the United States began the commercial enterprise in which the black body was transformed into a commodity to be traded in the public marketplace. The institutionalization of slavery naturalized in the social sphere the assumption of agency over the black body and everything it produced or laid claim to. After Reconstruction and with the rise of Jim Crow laws in the Deep South, this presumption continued as the legalized policing of black bodies in white space through political disenfranchisement, social segregation, and the more onerous legacy of lynch mobs. The project of minstrelsy as practiced by white performers simply reiterated this presumption of agency over the black body and introduced it into the cultural sphere as working-class entertainment. The objectification of blackness as popular commodity and the trade in insidious representations of blackness only inculcated a more deeply pejorative affect around black bodies in the American racial imagination as well as a great deal of ambivalence given the pleasures of racial play to be had. Nonetheless, the transfiguring effect of the staging of blackness onto white subjectivities that minstrelsy represented drew upon the black body as cultural capital but also as a consumer commodity that became increasingly disposable since its most desirable qualities could to some extent be replicated and mimicked, often deployed in subversive ways that challenged the status quo if not the social order.

Black culture, Deborah Root observes in her book *Cannibal Culture*, retains a cachet among contemporary white youth "increasingly uneasy about the emptiness and commodification of mainstream 'white-bread-culture,'" prompting them "to look elsewhere for meaning and cultural and aesthetic integrity"[1] but in ways that assume similar attitudes about agency instituted by minstrelsy. White appropriation of cultural, aesthetic, and spiritual traditions of ethnic and racial Others is problematic since they tend to "displace the local social, ceremonial, and political contexts of the cultural forms being appropriated,"[2] reducing substance to simulacra—commodity without context—but also because they tend to objectify the Other and naturalize difference. Consequently, the conceptual lines of escape out of Western culture and its stifling Victorianism into a titillating, yet manageable and pacified Other suggests a refusal "to come to terms with the continuing consequences of colonial histories,"[3] including the ways in which racial representation in popular culture have helped to perpetuate belief systems and social policies based on prejudice.

The sign of blackness may be viewed as a line of conceptual escape played out in the appropriation of black cultural and aesthetic expressions as commodity fetish created through mass-mediated forms of production. The interrogation of how this is the case does not necessarily suggest any "authentic" or essentialized blackness that can be despoiled. Nonetheless, as Root argues, only a cynical approach denies the possibility "of cultural practices having meaning in their original contexts, in a living social matrix"[4] connected to particular people in particular circumstances at particular historical moments. Commodity culture replaces people with objects and their histories with hegemonic narratives that obfuscate colonial oppression so that consumption becomes guiltless. It allows race and ethnicity to become resources for pleasure, and the cultures of repressed groups, as well as their bodies, come to be viewed as alternative playgrounds for members of dominant groups that "affirm their power-over in intimate relations with the Other."[5]

The body as a repository and transmitter of textual knowledge has played a critical yet overlooked role in the evolution of contemporary hip-hop as culture informed by a broad range of performance practices beyond the sound object. Arguably, the body has been as critical in the construction of the hip-hop community as have words and music. The body may be seen to represent another kind of constructed text that has, over the course of the culture's move from the periphery to the mainstream, been the nexus for all manner of cultural information critical in the construction of community and communal practices. That this is the case owes in no small part to the emergence of MTV at about the same time in the early 1980s, so that as hip-hop culture began to appear on the pop culture radar, the performance of the body was already a critical part of its appeal because of the foundational importance of the visually captivating art of b-boying.[6] MTV would inextricably bind the visual with material consumption and make both a part of youth culture in ways that previous entertainment/commercial technologies had not achieved. Anne Kaplan observes that MTV "more than other television, may be said to be *about* consumption," where unsatisfied desire becomes "displaced onto the record that will embody the star's magnetism and fascination."[7] There is no doubt that at least part of what is embedded within music videos becomes embedded in the music as well, but Kaplan misses a larger point here, though not by much. She implicitly alludes to the fact that the desire and illusion created by MTV are ultimately and most effectively displaced onto the performing body, since in video culture it is the performing body that is most central to retaining the performer's magnetism and fascination. The performing body has certainly been critical in the evolution of popular music and culture since minstrelsy, but with MTV it becomes more ubiquitous than ever. While it could have been said even relatively recently that the corporeal body as a site for cultural analysis was fairly understudied,[8] the body has increasingly become a site of intellectual and scholarly attention and an object of legitimate research for the social sciences. It now forms the basis for "the theoretical and empirical focus of a relatively novel subdiscipline, the 'sociology of the body,' and a concern for a wide range of sociological specialisms," including the sociology of sport and the emotions.[9]

Much emerging scholarship of the last two or three decades in particular has begun to focus on the black body in popular culture around issues of authenticity, agency, and appropriation. These kinds of projects are long overdue considering that Eric Lott in *Love and Theft* views blackface minstrelsy as "one of the very first constitutive discourses of the body in American culture,"[10] but whose study became inextricable from discussions around hegemonic repression and the legacy of Jim Crow. While it is certainly true that minstrelsy can be interpreted and contested as being about a great many things, it is first and foremost a practice of, on, and, to a good extent, about the corporeal body, the same of which may be said of contemporary practices in hip-hop culture that foreground the body as a critical site of performance. As hip-hop moved into the cultural mainstream, its most essential expressive features came to be articulated as modes of social and cultural performance by black males, so that constitutive practices of contemporary hip-hop have come to be largely defined by the perambulations of the black male body. A key difference in the ways these two musical practices originated and developed is certainly that minstrelsy located itself on white bodies and eventually came to be widely participated in by blacks, while hip-hop was largely located onto black bodies but is now widely participated in by whites and others as well. What scholarship around hip-hop cultural practices has yet to fully problematize is how other kinds of bodies—white bodies, Jewish bodies, Asian bodies, Native American bodies—become implicated in the appropriation and (re)presentation of whatever it is that blackness implies beyond ontology.

In the way that Scott Kiesling discusses how the term *dude* indexes for young white males a "stance of cool solidarity" as they navigate discourses around masculinity that demand group solidarity, demonstrable hetero-sexuality, and social nonconformity,[11] we can discuss the appropriation of the black male body in similar terms, as a textual space where young black males negotiate discourses of individual and group identity, power and differ-ence, desire and masculinity, coolness and belonging. As an index of hipness, the hip-hop body is anything but static; it is dynamic and fluid, signifying meaning that functions within a broader socio-cultural context. It is the nexus for many of the foundational cultural practices of hip-hop culture. Its agency must be accounted for in the same way that the agency of the city must be in discussing the relationship between themes such as sexual and social identity, globalization and nationalism, since cities "are not simply the empty containers or backdrops where social, economic and political events take place,"[12] but help to shape and define those events by virtue of demo-graphic, geographic, or other features that may be inherently unique. Black bodies, similarly, have never been empty containers of meaning. They have historically been integral to that process of organizing American coherence to which Toni Morrison refers, whether we mean in terms of our fractured body politic or our forms of cultural entertainment. In a racially bifurcated society, regardless of contestations around essentialism, they have enormous power to signify beyond pigmentation and phenotype, what Frantz Fanon refers to as the "fact of blackness."[13]

As Stuart Hall convincingly argues in *Race: The Floating Signifier*, race functions much like a language in that the meaning of race is relational and can shift depending on context since the meaning of a signifier is never fully, finally, or trans-historically fixed.[14] Blackness in hip-hop has been recast in terms of a transcultural and transnational identity mediated through sound, material culture, and the visual as well as through personal performance. It has become a signifier that inculcates ideas in particular about gender, race, identity, and urbanity at the site of the body. Hip-hop participants of various racial and ethnic backgrounds as social actors constitute a community of practice that has become fascinatingly diverse, and where stark affiliations may be telegraphed in very subtle displays and (re)negotiations of cultural codes. Nonetheless, while there is a body of recent scholarship that has begun to interrogate the modern encounter with the black body as a part of a hypermediated consumer culture, there remains a dearth of work that locates the white body and white subjectivity in popular culture as it becomes a site for the mediation and reproduction of blackness as social performance. In this transaction, a cultural transference takes place in which agency over black male bodies—and discourses *about* black male bodies—is contested, negotiated, and asserted by white social actors. For white adolescent males coming to terms with issues of masculinity and identity, the image of the swaggering black male in hip-hop videos is an appealing figure that has become iconic of an authentic and desirable representation of masculinity to be emulated. The caricatures of black male hip-hop gangsterism that white and other ethnic youth create for themselves through various affective strategies may be seen as metaphors "for one culture's ventriloquial self-expression through the art forms of someone else's."[15] What gets lost behind the imagery and masculine desire involved in the fetishization of the hip-hop gangster is the extent to which these representations of black masculinity depend upon and perpetuate the imagined malevolence of black males generally.

The black body and representations of black masculinity in hardcore styles of hip-hop performance are socially constructed kinds of gender and racial performance that are historically marked by notions around criminality, deviance, and pathology and that are deeply implicated in the construction of an African Americanized white masculinity mediated through popular culture media. Whites and other racial and ethnic groups who may have had little contact with black males except through such representations may find it difficult to see beyond the persona of the hardcore gangsta as performance, or in any case, as one kind of performance of black maleness that may be part real and part artifice. One problem with masculinity, in contrast to femininity, is certainly that it has largely remained imagined as "apparently unconstructed," and as such, "attempts to read masculinity as performance may be actually more difficult than seeing femininity as a construction."[16] Susan Bordo underscores this point in reminding us that men are not merely timeless symbolic constructs, but rather, are biologically, historically, and experientially embodied actors who are socially constructed over time and reconstructed at different historical moments.[17] Bordo's reading of the male body does not read race as carefully as it does gender and sexuality, but she is quite right in suggesting that as long as men are imagined to be transparent themselves, and if masculinity is not more closely interrogated, how then, can women have a real conversation with men around issues of gender? In a similar regard, if we do not interrogate the ways in which the black body remains "an ambiguous object in our society, still susceptible to whatever meanings the white gaze assigns to it," a cultural curiosity whose representations have historically been "interpreted, manipulated, and given to us, particularly in popular culture,"[18] discussions around the vagaries, contradictions, and consequences of racial performance are made extremely difficult.

Strategies in hardcore rap performance create extremely intensified affective investments in malevolence constructed in sound, lyrical choices, story narrative, and gestures of the body that confirm the most egregious discourses around black male deviancy in ways not previously seen in American popular music. Visual advertisements aimed at consumers of urban youth culture further complicate the trafficking of negatively affective imagery by using the bodies of black males to index hip-hop music and the performance of masculine power and aggression associated with it. Walking through a mall in Seattle, Washington, a few years ago, I was stopped by a lighted display box featuring a life-sized mean-mugging photo of the West Coast hardcore rapper The Game, wearing his just-released signature sneakers. The cold hardness in the facial expression, something near to vicious, made me wonder why any middle-class white parents would actually buy their kids these shoes if their only reference point was the unsettling image of a snarling, tattooed black thug looking back at them. Then I realized the kids probably have their own credit cards.

Nonetheless, standing there, beholding the image of The Game in all his commodified fury, I had flashes of the civil rights and black nationalist movements in the 1960s that represented watershed moments in which black males began to resist acceptable modes of social and emotional behavior, when the term *black rage* entered the lexicon of public discourse around race, rights, and social resistance, embodied in the faces of men like Stokely Carmichael and Huey Newton. It occurred to me how black rage, the backlash of years of pent-up black indignation over racial oppression that finally erupted into street marches and flaming buildings had become just another marketing tool to hawk sneakers. Nor does such advertising necessarily suggest the rise of a "post-racist" culture in which such representations of black males are tolerated and accepted. Rather, the kind of commodity racism they inculcate merely breeds and perpetuates more pejorative views of black males and, arguably, black people generally. For consumers of hip-hop and urban street culture they may indeed arouse desire, but for other segments of society such images only serve to proliferate feelings of racial hostility that become particularly displaced onto black male bodies without discrimination. Since one of the most insidious manners in which the objectifying gaze infuses American culture is "in people's encounters with visual media that spotlight bodies and body parts,"[19] visual performance in hardcore hip-hop imagery is highly problematic when it comes to this kind of objectification because it can be consumed without other kinds of ameliorating cross-racial social interactions.

In hardcore styles of hip-hop, facial expressions are used to telegraph hypermasculinity and ideals of physical and psychic hardness that are critical in the construction of performers' persona. It is this "relative facial prominence"[20] of emotional stoicism that helps to project masculine power while simultaneously self-objectifying the performer. Representations of masculinity in hip-hop also focus on "body-ism"[21] in the same way that the body is prioritized in sexual objectification. The wearing of ostentatious jewelry, including expensive chains, earrings, and "grillz" (full-frontal dental overlays, often made of gold and encrusted with diamonds), tattoos, stylized athletic apparel or brand-name urban street wear, as well as the display of the shirtless torso are ways that visually display masculine power and sexuality by privileging the objectified and spectacularized body.

The (re)circulation of representations of urban black males that reify the ideal of hypermasculine hardness has also become a multidimensional index that distinguishes the grittier, more graphic, and provocative styles of hardcore rap that appeared in the 1980s (new school) from earlier (old school) styles of 1970s party rap.[22] What these representations commodify and (re)present back to adolescent males are essentially decontextualized images, codes, and symbols around what it means to be black, male, and authentic in an urban environment; qualities that include emotional rigidity, a rejection of the feminine acted out in misogynistic behavior, nihilism, and an adherence to a code of the street that prioritizes illicit material gain, ostentatious consumption and the defense of territory defined as both personal and geographical space. As these music styles and lifestyles moved from the cultural borderlands into mainstream culture through the 1990s, the association between harder styles of rap music and violence came to be embodied by the young black male, who was seen "as exotic, dangerous, and feared, yet simultaneously appealing and marketable."[23]

The expression of rage and the withholding of emotions that suggest vulnerability by black males in hardcore rap culture may arguably be seen as recuperative, as oppositional strategies that push back against the emasculation of black masculinity where assertiveness and the expression of sovereign masculinity were sanctioned. The protest movements of the 1950s and 1960s took shape as African Americans began to openly resist normative, acceptable modes of social and emotional behavior. As the term *black rage* entered the lexicon of public discourse, more complexly nuanced expressions of black emotion challenged white patriarchal power relationships. Certainly more nihilistic and apolitical than 1960s black nationalism, hardcore hip-hop practices give new aesthetic expression to black urban rage by engaging an array of oppositional strategies, including the aggressive performance of the body, the dense layering of discordant sonic textures, incendiary and obscene language, violent narratives of urban nihilism, and distinctive styles of vernacular urban dress that are read as subversive. The expression of objectionable emotion and aggressive behavior in hardcore hip-hop performance has helped to reshape ideas around masculinity and authenticity so that for many young males even the act of smiling is seen as registering weakness, feminization, and relative lower social status. The performance of hardcore masculinity rejects the softening of one's facial features in favor of the cold, hard stare intended to project strength and inspire fear if not respect.

Simon Frith has made a number of important observations regarding the affective nature of the body and its role in constructing musical performance that is a social, communicative process where "the musician's body is also an instrument"[24] that articulates a rhetoric of physical gestures—movements of the body and hands, facial expression, posture, and adornment—and which mark the body as a site of narrative and of feeling. Speech patterns are particularly important in this regard in hip-hop, because they help to (re)construct the inner-city street as a site of performance and constant self-dramatization. As Frith suggests, "the most significant linguistic source of performing conventions is undoubtedly 'talking black,' the 'speaking behavior' of African-American and African-Caribbean communities," but it is also "the everyday experience of vernacular performance which has made African-American culture so important as a source of popular performing expertise, of popular performing style,"[25] and that forms much of what have become articulations of American popular cultural expression.

The fetishism of racial reproduction inherent in these appropriations and the ways in which tropes of blackness become dislocated onto other kinds of bodies as performance and personal identity produce an "affective value"[26] that operates alongside systems of economic, symbolic, and cultural values as another way of understanding the world. The body, as the primary site for these transactions of personal style and expressive behavior, acts as a vehicle for implied metaphors around blackness and black male behavior that are subsumed as normal and naturalized. They become performances of the everyday in a new kind of masculine culture that is analogous to but in many respects very different from past macho-racial transactions of this kind. For one thing, racial desire is much more culturally pervasive and socially accepted, which only reaffirms its cachet as a kind of transcultural currency in the global marketplace. Theorizing the meaning of the black male body and the ways it is represented in popular culture has begun partly as a result of global corporate commodification, where the black body "intermittently emerges as a signifier of prestige, autonomy, transgression, and power in a supranational economy of signs"[27] that is increasingly complex.

Since minstrelsy, blackness has been one of America's primary cultural exports, a tool to sell everything from sheet music depicting grotesque representations of African Americans to sneakers endorsed by an authentic street thug. Ahmed Ertegun, the founder of Atlantic Records, remarked shortly before his death that black American music is the only popular music style that travels around the world and becomes adopted and adapted by other countries and cultures. It is not that he is saying other musical styles do not travel and become localized, but that they rarely become so integrated into the fabric of a culture as have black music and other expressive cultural productions. Black American music and its derivatives in rock have laid the foundation for much of the popular music styles in cultures across the globe where contact with indigenous influences have also produced any number of hybridized forms. It travels through sound and technologies of sound recording and distribution and also as representation produced by the technologies of visual media culture. It has also traveled through ideologies of race that have perhaps been understudied insofar as they have influenced how others in the world perceive, consume, appropriate, and learn to relate to black Americans and black American culture. Blackness, argues E. Patrick Johnson, is a site of cross-cultural appropriation that has provided fertile ground upon which to formulate new epistemologies of self and Other. As such, performance is useful not only in studying blackness, but blackness is quite useful in studying performance since both are discourses whose histories converge at the site of Otherness. Racist constructions of blackness associate it with denigration, impurity, and nature, while the devaluation of performance in Western intellectual traditions simultaneously coincides with the devaluation of black people as subjects of inquiry in the academy and in society. Traditions of black performance that privilege the body such as music, dance, and speech are reduced to "spectacles of primitivism"[28] to justify the postcolonial gaze.

The complaints of African American participants in hip-hop culture whose claims to cultural agency and authorship—as opposed to ownership—are being erased as a process of global commodification and appropriation is perhaps akin to the appropriation in eighteenth-century England of the carnivalesque by bourgeoisie nobility. The English elite discursively reformed what had been a subversive practice by the lower class, where "the grotesque body of the carnival" was re-territorialized, appropriated, sublimated, and individualized to code refined upper-class identity. It gave nobility and the bourgeoisies the masks and symbols of a kind of liberatory freedom of expression "at the very moment when they were repudiating the social realm from which those masks and symbols came."[29] These symbols were systematically severed from the lives of the working class and transformed into forms of vicarious pleasure for the elite that transgressed lines of sex and class. Black cultural production appropriated by mainstream American culture finds similar routes of escape coming from those blacks existing at the margins of society, which since the 1960s have been privileged sites of authenticity by social researchers.

The Swedish urban anthropologist Ulf Hannerz argued that the writings of the African American sociologist E. Franklin Frazier in the 1930s and 1940s on black families in urban settings foregrounded much of the work that would be conducted on black life in the 1960s. Hannerz believed that in Frazier's work, "the lower class black family allegedly reverted, with matrifocality, to a primitive evolutionary stage,"[30] and that later studies took up this viewpoint in a variety of ways that essentialized perspectives of black masculinity to the underclass.[31] Hannerz's own study is based on fieldwork conducted in poor sections of Washington, D.C., in 1966 and 1968, in which he attempts to "outline the social processes within the ghetto communities of the northern United States whereby the identity of street corner males is established and maintained."[32] In his study, *What Ghetto Males Are Like: Another Look*, Hannerz writes that the "emphasis on the socio-economic matrix of family life which Frazier's work foreshadowed has emerged as the third major perspective in black American family studies, and this point of view is now probably dominant."[33]

In the search for black authenticity, particularly in the wake of the Kerner Commission report in 1968,[34] all roads apparently led to the ghetto, which, at the end of the day, remained unchanged. The failure of the Johnson administration's War on Poverty to fully address issues of deep poverty and economic disenfranchisement among inner-city blacks and the further retrenchment by later administrations on civil rights era gains, along with other factors such as urban decay and the social marginalization of a generation of black youth, helped set the stage for the emergence of hip-hop's ghettocentric street ethos in the late 1970s. The poverty and desperation among inner-city black youth also ripened conditions for the rise of street drug gangs in the 1980s and the emergence of the hardcore gangsta figure, who was essentially a reincarnation of the folkloric bad nigger and whose foray into hip-hop turned the ghetto into a surrealistic playground of racial fantasy for adolescent suburban males. White consumers of the kind of hardcore rap that began to penetrate popular music in the late 1980s and the early 1990s traffic the same back alleyways of Norman Mailer's 1950s white hipster, who romanticizes the black male as underclass antihero and revels "in the worst of perversion, promiscuity, pimpery, drug addiction, rape, razor-slash, bottle-break, what-have-you."[35] In what Mailer characterizes as a "morality of the bottom," his hipsters reject the mores of Victorian decorum in search of the indiscreet pleasures to be had from racial transgression, "looking for action with a black man's code to fit their facts."[36] Nor is the adoption of these representations in hip-hop culture limited to white youth in the United States; it is now a global pandemic.

In her study of "Blasians" ("black Asians"), Japanese youth who attempt to identify with black American culture through performative gestures associated with hip-hop, visual artist iona rozeal brown presents an intriguing commentary on the intersection of Japanese culture and African American hip-hop culture by introducing the blackface mask of the minstrel into the equation. brown traveled to Japan to meet and paint some of these youth, who adopt such affectations as oversized gold chains, the black fedoras worn by Run-DMC, cornrow hairstyles, afro-puffs, and baggy clothing often worn along with traditional Japanese clothing as well as such mannerisms as crotch-grabbing and the flashing of gang signals. brown's study powerfully suggests how the body becomes the text in which the visual is played out through coded gestures of meaning even when those gestures are decontextualized and culturally decentered. The bodies of Blasians become playgrounds for gender and racial fantasy for youth who may have seen few representations of black Americans other than the crude imagery of the hardcore rap videos they attempt to emulate. brown's use of masking signifies on the racial masquerade at play when youth (re)construct representations of the hyper-masculine and hypersexual black male (and the hypersexual black female) through spectacularized dress and physical gestures.

Michael Awkward discusses these kinds of racial performances in terms of "transraciality" that necessitates a radical revision of one's own natural markings and the adoption of aspects of the human surface, particularly skin, hair, and facial and other distinctive features associated with the racial Other. The transgression opens a space for altering the experience of one's racial designation in exchange for another and exposes "the constructedness of the rules of racial being."[37] We can begin to see how the black body becomes a kind of discursive text inscribed with an array of possible meanings that become appropriated and performed by other kinds of bodies in ways that signify powerful historical ideologies about black male deviance, criminality, and sexuality. These kinds of articulations become even more complex when we acknowledge that all youth attempt to find ways of self-expression outside of hegemonic social codes that would otherwise define them, so that the embracing of black identities by nonblack actors may certainly in some cases be seen as attempts to subvert social and racial hierarchies. David Samuels writes that Carl Van Vechten's 1926 best-selling novel *Nigger Heaven,* for example, "imagined a masculine, criminal, yet friendly black ghetto world that functioned . . . as a refuge from white middle-class boredom."[38] White jazzman Milton "Mezz" Mezzrow, on the other hand, claimed that his intimacy with black people in Harlem had physically transformed him into a Negro, whose sensibilities he had come to share. In both cases, Samuels argues, "by inverting the moral values attached to contemporary racial stereotypes, Van Vechten and Mezzrow at once appealed to and sought to undermine the prevailing racial order."[39] Such practices continue to be complexly contradictory if occasionally exasperating in the logic of racial transvesting that they employ, even more so when they produce no real cross-racial discourse, amelioration of racial attitudes, or changes in the structural causes of racial inequality.

Rap music performance's signifying practices may likewise be liberating and subversive, but even so, they rely on fantasies of the racialized Other and idealized tropes of racial deviance in the pursuit of identity, meaning, and pleasure. In this regard, such fantasies perhaps unwittingly fall into the trap of racist ideologies implicated in punitive censorship of the black body in white space. Deborah Wong has noted how rap, as a transnational popular music genre, has become "a site where the body and ground (i.e., history, community) can come into conflict"[40] in terms of race and ethnicity since it is a music rooted in African American performance practices but that has been adopted by participants in other global communities where a coherent understanding of black American culture remains scant. The centrality of hip-hop culture to any number of global youth cultures, then, does not necessarily suggest empathy with or recognition of black American culture since the kind of racial information that is being transmitted is likely to be reductive or problematic.

Hip-hop music and culture have been integral in the construction of a new cultural complex of racial perceptions about black masculinity and the black male body that may be viewed instead in terms of dislocation and decontextualization. Ideas about black masculinity relocated and transposed not simply to other geographical locations, but onto other kinds of bodies are reinscribed in representations that reproduce and perpetuate pejorative understandings of black subjectivities. This process exposes the social constructedness and fluidity of concepts of race as well as the perpetuation of racialized thinking through cultural forms of representation and the institutions that support them. It becomes crucial, then, to mark how racial objectification and performance are constructed and transferred across cultural and social borders, and how they inform ideas about racial desire played out in the crucible of youthful pleasure.

In the following chapter, I explore a number of ways of looking at and thinking about the body, objectification, and performance in the context of hip-hop and its particular aesthetics, and the ways in which they have manifested themselves over time through an array of cultural productions.

# 3. Affective Gestures

## Hip-hop Aesthetics, Blackness, and the Literacy of Performance

In hip-hop culture, uniqueness and the expression of individual identity are prioritized through behavior, modes of dress, language, and other ways. Even when styles and expressive behaviors are emulated, imitated, and adopted by those wishing to identify with the culture, they are often at some point adapted and signified upon—there are those who innovate and those who "bite" (appropriate) the innovations of others. In this way, expressive behaviors continue to evolve, continually creating something new from something old, always seeking that which is "fresh."[1] These styles and behaviors are conveyed by cultural trendsetters, whether they have name recognition through visual media and high-volume record sales or are underground artists with street buzz. Those who adopt these styles of behavior in mannerism, dress, speech, or attitude become part of a community of practice that is able to persist because the expressive codes associated with the culture have the power to invoke it through any number of performative texts. I use the term *text* in the broadest possible sense, or as in the "world as text,"[2] where everything is encoded with meaning that must be deciphered, read, and interpreted. Thus the discursive practices involved in hip-hop that become mastered by one person are eventually passed on until a community of adherents is established. In the case of consumers of hip-hop culture who do not have access to "native speakers," those from whom the music and cultural innovations come, electronic mediation becomes the basis for appropriating the texts and symbols around which they form their own communities of practice as well as their own interpretations of these texts and symbols.

Texts are themselves socially constructed linguistic artifacts that in a reflexive way act to help (re)imagine social identity and social community, so that the idea of "textual communities"[3] helps explain the connection between literary culture and the imagining of community, where community centers not only around literal textual documents, but around literate interpreters of these texts. As Brian Stock suggests in *The Implications of Literacy*, communities may be constructed and guided by certain texts that need not be physically present as long as they exist—and their meanings are agreed upon—in the minds of those who comprise the community. Word of mouth can construct "a superstructure of an agreed meaning" that is ultimately internalized, and this is true also of images and other affective gestures that become extended beyond the original person or group.[4] Stock's observations are extremely relevant to the study of hip-hop culture and how it has passed from the margins to the center of American and global youth culture. The texts that construct the culture constitute a kind of literacy that has now been largely internalized by youth worldwide to form a community of practice that identifies with hip-hop as a social and/or cultural movement or merely as a means of interpersonal interaction and pleasure.

This literacy is not only a literacy of music and rhetoric but a literacy of the body and the visual. The body as a repository of textual knowledge and as a transmitter of that knowledge has played as important a role in transferring information about the cultural dynamics of hip-hop as have mix tapes of words and music videos. The textual elements found in hip-hop culture involve "processes of social mapping that provide the coordinates for charting issues and practices within the broad terrains of popular culture."[5] It is not so much that the notion of an authentic urban black identity is encapsulated in hip-hop culture as a whole since even urban black identities are quite diverse, but that the culture of the street does provide social texts that make sense to black male youth who dwell in urban environments and who identify with the codes and meanings that emanate from various subcultures within hip-hop, for example, prison culture, street gangs, and hustlers. Since these texts are now largely consumed through the global diffusion of electronic media and have been broadly appropriated in many parts of the world, youth in virtually any geographical location can construct personal identity and localized meaning around hip-hop music and cultural practices, including the performance of masculinity derived from the mass-mediated posturings of black American males.

## Mediascape of Hip-hop Aesthetics and Performance Practices

Hip-hop has been transmitted and interpreted by all manner of textual media—as songs traded as mix tapes, as commercially produced and distributed records and CDs, as music videos and cinematic film, and as advertisement displays, as well as in magazines and on Internet websites. These all act as kinds of constructed texts by which the socio-political and cultural values, attitudes, alliances, musical tastes, and visual style associated with hip-hop have spread globally. In *The Cosmopolitan Vernacular*, Sheldon Pollock addresses "the mutually constitutive relationship of literature and community" in which literature calls into being particular "socio-textual communities."[6] The community of practices that allows the formation of a separate and distinct group or for some loosely affiliated hip-hop nation acts in the same way as does literature in this regard, by becoming the textual basis that binds this community together. It is in community that people become socialized, develop kinship relations and friendships, and learn to recognize the boundaries of those social relations as well as various stylistic practices that become replicated within it. The texts of rap vocal performances—the narratives, language, and vernacular expressions of young black males that are constructed of a diverse range of overlapping cultural productions—have become for many in this community performances that construct social and personal identity.

Performance, which may include "everywhere in life, from ordinary gestures to macrodramas,"[7] often involves the construction of a *personal front* that is part of the expressive equipment that a person deploys in performance of self and social identity. This equipment includes the items that we most intimately identify with the performer himself and that we naturally expect will follow the performer wherever he goes, items that may include insignia of office or rank; clothing; sex, age, and racial characteristics; size and looks; posture; speech patterns; facial expressions; bodily gestures; and the like.[8] Many of these performative gestures in hip-hop culture can be mapped graphically to demonstrate how they interact and intersect so that some of the aesthetic, social, and cultural choices that make up these gestures can be identified and viewed visually. I have drawn from a visual schematic proposed by cultural anthropologist Robert Plant Armstrong[9] in his study of Yoruba art and consciousness entitled *The Affecting Presence*, in which he discusses the way in which affect (feeling), signifiers, and performance practices are expressed across a range of expressive aesthetic vehicles, including music, dance, drama, poetry, sculpture, graphic arts, architecture, costume, and verbal narrative.[10] These aesthetic expressions, Armstrong argues, reveal the "externalization of man's interiority—an actuality of human experience" and attempt to prove that "art is man living" not simply through creation, but *as* creation. Reflecting on *The Affecting Presence* in his subsequent work *Wellspring*,[11] he suggests two other problems that concerned him in the former work, which were "to identify some of the revealing physical features of the work of art, showing their cultural variability. I wanted to show art as a phenomenon of man writ whole and large. In the second place, I wanted to describe the range of these parameters and to reveal in depth some of the art of particular people."[12]

Armstrong indexes performance practices through a number of what he calls *affecting media* that are highly interpretive and rely on variable uses of situation (particular context), surface, color, volume, tone, movement, word, relationality (relative context), and experience (personal life experience or group experience). These things are always implied in performance, and the degree to which any one of them is used determines individual style, a performer's particular "flava," or way of organizing and interpreting essentially the same elements to arrive at a different result. As Armstrong writes, "the media of the affecting presence are the minima of presentationality. They lie this side of the basic cultural consciousness which they bear. The real medium of the affecting presence therefore is consciousness itself, freighted into color, tone, volume, surface, movement, word and situation."[13] The idea that it is consciousness that provides the cultural basis for aesthetic choices and innovation in black urban arts has been meticulously detailed with respect to rap music by ethnomusicologist Cheryl Keyes in *Rap Music and Street Consciousness,* in which she traces the music's evolution back to jive talk radio DJs, black nationalist activists like H. Rap Brown, and literary provocateurs like the playwright LeRoi Jones and his black arts movement, which existed from the mid-1960s to the mid-1970s. The black arts movement was Jones' effort to create a consciously "revolutionary" art that would "get into the street, that would reach our people," and where poetic skills, for example, "were not judged on rhyme per se but rather on one's ability to articulate themes relevant to African American life."[14] Out of this experiment came any number of expressive practices and poetic voices including Harlem's The Last Poets, recognized by hip-hop pioneers such as Afrika Bambaataa as "the first or original style rappers."[15] The consciousness-raising efforts of the black arts movement would help to fuel the rise of hip-hop's subversive street aesthetics, its early socio-political undertone, its foundational performance practices such as b-boying and the art of the DJ,[16] and an ongoing, organic dynamic to keep innovating and creating something fresh from something old, a dynamic that drives hip-hop even now. This dynamic is not only expressed in music, dance, and poetics, but in a multitude of other ways that incorporate adornment of the physical body, the use of public space, and the performance of self through alter-egos and assumed identities so that participants in the culture, whether performers or consumers, are able to express themselves as Armstrong suggests, not simply *through* the creation of art, but *as* art manifested as themselves.

I have transposed Armstrong's aesthetic forms (see Table 1) to comparable expressive forms in what are generally accepted to be the four primary pillars of hip-hop culture—b-boying (dance), graffiti art (graphic art), beats (music), and rhyming (poetics),[17] practices that are all quite diverse and multifaceted—and other expressive practices in hip-hop that have to do with space and place (rather than architecture),[18] drama (a similar meaning in the sense of dramatic stories drawn from life experience), flow (verbal narrative as unique vocal style), and gear (costume), which together construct a comprehensive "musickal" performance.[19] Finally, where Armstrong uses sculpture as one kind of aesthetic expressive form, I have substituted the body to emphasize how in hip-hop culture it is used as an expressive medium in a variety of ways. Together, then, these offer a visual way in which to examine the corporeal body and its cultural productions in hip-hop culture as a moving collection of signifiers played out in an arena of musical and social performance. In *Watching Race: Television and the Struggle for Blackness*, media sociologist Herman Gray uses the term *mediascape* to describe the way in which within contemporary consumer culture "black youth constantly use the body, self-adornment, movement, language, and music to construct and locate themselves socially and culturally"[20] through an array of performative gestures. I have adopted this as a useful term, but I am using it a little differently. While Gray applies the term to popular mass media such as television, film, and advertising, I use it to refer to my organization of affecting media and hip-hop aesthetics. My theorizing about how the mediascape functions, however, is closer to what Gray intends, which is "to situate black youth subjectivities at the center of popular cultural analysis"[21] and to capture some of "the flavor—the dialogue and hybridity—of black youth practices and inventions"[22] in a more visual way in order to show some of the intersections and

*Table 1.* Mediascape of Hip-hop Cultural Aesthetics and Performance Practices

| | Body | B-Boying | Graffiti | Beats | Space/Place | Drama | Flow | Gear | Rhymes |
|---|---|---|---|---|---|---|---|---|---|
| Situation | X | X | X | X | X | X | X | X | X |
| Surface | X | | X | | X | | X | | |
| Color | X | | X | | X | | X | | |
| Volume | X | | X | X | X | | X | X | |
| Tone | X | X | X | X | X | X | X | X | X |
| Movement | X | X | X | X | X | X | X | X | |
| Word | X | | X | X | X | X | X | X | X |
| Relationality | X | X | X | X | X | X | X | X | X |
| Experience | X | X | X | X | X | X | X | X | X |

The body and aesthetic aspects of performance intersect and interact with variable features including relationality and experience, producing new interpretations and fresh approaches to established practices.

interplay that these practices construct. I also share Gray's understanding of the importance of the body, that it "seems to reign as the preeminent site for the expression of individual imagination and collective cultural identity"[23] in black youth culture and certainly in hip-hop culture.

Table 1 visually shows the interrelatedness of expressive structural forms and the ways that individual play and aesthetic signifying through various mediated elements produce what is highly prized as fresh, as a new twist on an old idea or a uniquely different way of doing something. *Flava* is constructed out of various combinations of media acting on expressive forms in hip-hop, and where they are organized differently by each person in terms of his or her experience. *Experience*, in turn, informs the *relationality* of these media to the expressive forms, since no two people will necessarily bring the same kind of *situational*, or life, experience and wordplay to the practice of rhyming, graffiti writing, b-boying, or other ways of self-expression in hip-hop culture, a fact that can readily be seen in the vast array of individual styles and practices that since the early 1990s have produced what Gray characterizes as "a powerful counter-hegemonic force in the cultural politics of American society."[24] The fact of this cultural counterforce and its subsequent evolution into a political force is nowhere more obvious than in the 2008 election of Barack Obama, the nation's first hip-hop president, and of whom I will speak more in later pages.

As Armstrong makes clear, each intersection of form and media has the potential to articulate something in innumerable ways so that virtually no element ever exists in isolation. The range of affective signifiers that play on the surface of the body—from ostentatious jewelry, tattoos, and stylized athletic apparel to gestures and movements—help to contextualize them and may all be seen as relational, meaning they are not isolated from other expressive gestures. Bodies, music, rhymes, space/place, clothing, and so forth may all be discussed as having and giving off a certain *tone* when we move that word away from a musical terminology related to sound, pitch, and timbre, to indicate terms such as character, quality, manner, and attitude. The terms *relationality, experience, situation,* and *tone* are in some way defining features in virtually every expressive act, social relationship, and gesture in hip-hop's cultural milieu. It is the way in which these are all deployed as integrated and interrelated aspects of hip-hop music and culture that is implicated in the construction of individual identity and personal style. Viewed in this way, it may become clear how various aspects of hip-hop expressive culture function as kinds of discourse, as an accumulation of signs and imagery emanating from black American urban popular culture through a globalized, multinational, and multimediated culture industry. They offer aesthetic ideals and ways of self-expression that can be created and consumed in the absence of any real contact with black people, a fact that has created considerable tensions along lines of race and class and around issues of agency and authenticity over the last quarter century. While not attempting to exhaust the myriad of possibilities for interpreting this table, I will nonetheless discuss a few aspects of it which are to me of particular importance.

## Space Is the Place

As I have suggested, the four traditional pillars of hip-hop do not in themselves sufficiently suggest all of the aesthetic dimensions and dynamics at play in the culture and the multitude of ways in which they are related and can be performed to express something personal and unique. Space and place, for instance, are relational to all expressive forms, since they are the creative zones where expressive behaviors take place. Mediated references to place and space allow those who do not live in geographical zones where black expressive behavior is part of the performance of the everyday to re-create spaces of racialized play outside these zones.[25] In *The 'Hood Comes First: Race, Space, and Place in Rap and Hip-Hop*, Murray Forman has demonstrated how space and place have acted as sites of memory and history in hip-hop culture. Rap performers often name themselves after the streets, neighborhoods or area codes where they grew up, a practice also used by street taggers at the dawning of hip-hop who spray-painted their names on open walls and, later, on the sides of commuter trains in New York City. Often, gestures of remembrance for deceased friends are painted on walls in public spaces as words or elaborate murals, reaffirming the importance of the link between history, memory, and the sense of place. In a literal sense, Forman suggests, "the street has been a consistent site for emergent hip-hop practices: block parties, break-dancing, and graffiti are all strongly associated with forms of expression that occur in outdoor or unsanctioned public spaces. This historical grounding in the authority of the street has had important implications for hip-hop throughout its evolution, providing a thread between contemporary practices and the formative practices upon which they are founded."[26]

Space and place in particular have become critical in contemporary hip-hop culture since the late 1980s, when the emergence of gangsta rap performers articulated and privileged certain geographical locales as territorial zones, not that this practice did not already exist around the boroughs of New York.[27] Spatial referents in hip-hop lore since the 1980s typically indicate specific geographical references to certain of these spaces—the Bronx, Queens, Brooklyn, Compton, 8-Mile Road, the "Yay Area" (San Francisco

Bay), or the "Dirty South." These places are in fact quite diverse in many ways, but at least in hardcore narratives, there is an association with the street and with certain kinds of activity and social engagement among young urban black males that are often illicit and transgressive. Therefore, the black urban ghetto occupies a central position in urban rap narratives and is richly encoded, but is also a space of great ambivalence as well as malevolence. It is, on the one hand, Jeremy Bentham's Panopticon recast as a site that is economically and racially segregated and policed to ensure the permanent visibility of its inhabitants, and consequently a certain control over them; it is a form of containment that "assures dissymmetry, disequilibrium, and difference."[28] On the other hand, if the black ghetto as an urban geographical space in American cities evolved out of a system of segregation and race-based residential allocation that permitted no freedom of choice, it also became "the one place where blacks have had the freedom to engage in expressive behavior without undue interference"[29] and within which black folk culture is learned, transmitted, and preserved as a set of values and behaviors different from both the dominant culture and black middle-class culture. These urban enclaves represent the continuation of black working-class folkways from the rural South, what G. M. Lewis refers to as "the Negro culture sphere"[30] which has been responsible for an abundance of African American aesthetic production.

The development of black ghetto culture and patterns of localized social behavior in northern cities, particularly after World War II, reflect a lifestyle repertoire that has historically supported people transplanted from the South to an urban milieu that subsequently encouraged their own uniquely urbanized culture spheres. Contemporary urban space—the inner city, the ghetto, the 'hood—became associated with notions of authenticity and blackness, and with class, which continue to be articulated in a variety of ways. The nomenclature of the 'hood has marked space and place as not only geographically defined locations, but also as idealized loci of personal, social, and cultural interactions that negotiate a particular kind of black urban identity and associates it with authenticity. To be a "real nigga" in rap music parlance is to be a product of the ghetto, a political move that implicitly acknowledges the limitations of American democracy, the failure of post–civil rights era racial politics, and black middle-class abandonment. For many white middle-class consumers of gangsta rap, on the other hand, the black ghetto "is a place of adventure, unbridled violence, erotic fantasy, and/or an imaginary alternative to suburban boredom"[31] made more readily available with the dramatic rise of commodity (re)production of black popular culture through magazines, music videos, films, video games, and apparel since the early 1990s.

## Lean Back and Swagga:
## The Black Body in Performance

The black male body and its signifying role in this matrix of cultural productions that is hip-hop remains a highly contested though relatively understudied site of performance in popular culture studies, but it is useful for two reasons. First, the black male body can be used to interrogate the male body as a site for the examination of the sociology of masculinity, of hierarchical forms of masculinity as privileged and powerful, and of assumptions about sexual and gender superiority because in doing so we may "come to some appreciation of how dominant discourses act upon bodies in a performative yet material manner."[32] Second, while the notion of a singular black masculinity is problematic since "it can be used to 'naturalize' difference between black and white men,"[33] it is nonetheless true that black male bodies in American culture have been marked as hypervisual sites of hypersexuality and hypermasculinity. The negative social implications of these representations and the fact they are nonetheless indexed as touchstones of hipness, coolness, and social rebellion celebrated through imitation appear highly contradictory. Since the black male body in this context is constantly in motion and highly organic, moving through any number of discursive fields and thus redefining itself in different places and at different times, the body-ism at play in hip-hop culture can be read as highly situational. We are often asked to read it in the context of historical and contemporary stereotypes of black males that are seen as naturalized rather than socially constructed and performative.

Judith Halberstam has demonstrated how subject the body is to the fluidity of performance and interpretation by focusing on the construction of feminine masculinity in drag king culture, which positions the female body in a highly situational context in which we are asked to read it as male. The drag king body is highly contextualized, encoded with affective markers such as facial hair and traditional male attire that provide a masculine counter-narrative to the body's presumed gender location as feminine. This is very much in the spirit of the carnivalesque and the transgressive since "the cultural practices of drag, cross-dressing, and the sexual stylization of butch/femme identities" interrogates and subverts the idea of an original or primary gender identity through parody and performance.[34] Such performances can be read as either degrading or uncritically appropriative of sex-role stereotyping, but when we consider how white and other social actors engage gender and race in hip-hop performance, we find similar processes at play. Drag kings use parody to play upon "the distinction between the anatomy of the performer and the gender that is being performed,"[35] while white males doing gangsta drag may or may not inadvertently parody historical stereotypes of hyper-sexuality, hypermasculinity, social aggression, and criminality as well as the variety of stylized ways of social interaction associated with black males.

In hip-hop, the body is privileged through motion and gesture that subvert the regulation of the bourgeois body and its normative vertical axis, wherein the lower bodily stratum is regulated or denied. The body in hip-hop not only subverts ordinary clothing attire by reframing, the most iconic example of which is the reverse-turned baseball cap, but also subverts Victorian models of proper decorum by articulating new representations of body posture, move-ment, and gesture much as jazz musicians have done historically. Movement, gesture, posture, and kinds of stylized street wear are discourses that mark many young urban black males in full rebellion against standard norms of deportment, and draw from a vernacular vocabulary of stylized expressive movement that black youth have used to mark difference. In the 1960s, the gait referred to at the time as the so-called pimp walk, affected by springing from one foot to the other with one hand and arm held closely to the side, was not all that uncommon among urbane and hip young black males. The mainstay of this walking is "rhythm and style," as are other expressions of "nonverbal styling," including body stance,[36] handshakes, and eye work "that black youth often deploy as strategies to set themselves apart."[37] Handshakes represent a special set of movements, usually ritualized, associated with black male performativity, which continue over time and which have become absorbed into the lexicon of hand greetings used uniformly by many youth. In the past, giving "dap," a vernacular expression for a ritualized hand greeting or farewell, included variations such as "slapping five," "giving skin," "high-fives," or the "soul shake," involving the gripping of thumbs. Such gestures indexed mascu-linity, community, and identity as part of a socio-cultural aesthetic associated with soul music in the 1960s.[38] One gesture, certainly, that has survived from the 1960s to the present and that is ubiquitous particularly in hardcore hip-hop performance is the rather crude act of crotch-grabbing, which not only emphasizes the lower bodily stratum that Victorianism denies, but provokes with the threat of sexual aggression that black males have been so historically assailed. The obscene nature of the act can be interpreted in a variety of ways when deployed by various people, but arguably, in the case of hardcore rap performance, for example, it telegraphs defiance to a race-based social order in which black masculinity has historically been contained and emasculated.

Other contemporary gestures in hip-hop are highly individualized and regional, and are constantly being updated. Since the late 1980s, they have also been infiltrated by numerous hand signs and other gestures that index urban street gang affiliation in a number of geographical locations. Hand signals can form crude representations of letters that spell out one's membership in one of the numerous sets that exist within the Crips, Bloods, or other street gangs. What would appear to be dance movements as well, such as the step movement referred to as the "Crip Walk," or "Blood Walk," may be used to spell out letters and communicate in coded ways that combine body gesture and the relationality of words and their usage. There are numerous variations and a vocabulary of movements in these once secretive movements and patterns that continue to expand. Once guarded, they have been widely circulated in music videos and can be found on various online websites performed by known rappers, gang members, and amateurs. Snoop Dogg, who often uses his music to acknowledge his Crips affiliation, rather brazenly illustrated steps taken from the routine in his CD release entitled *R&G: Rhythm n' Gangsta: The Masterpiece*. A search of the Internet video site *YouTube* turned up thousands of homemade video recordings of Crip Walk and Blood Walk variations. These very evocative interpretive dances, which still carry some risk of consequence depending upon the context in which they are performed, situate the performing body within the context of a particular gang or a particular gang-set. The availability of these dances has moved them out of their street gang–affiliated contexts and into global popular culture, where they further associate gang culture and the performing black male body with notions of masculinity and authenticity in hardcore rap culture.

The idea of *street swagger* updates the idea of physical motion, cool pose, and attitude. It is to some degree both an external and an internal act of performance, as it indexes not only rhythm and style in one's performance of physical self and personal carriage, but also suggests a high degree of self-confidence, the knowledge that one can handle himself in any situation with cool and sophistication. It also suggests the sense of empowerment that comes with success, however that is measured, and with getting respect from one's peers, associates, and others. Black jazz musicians may have historically indexed a kind of coolness in style and demeanor that became essential to the masculine performance of hipness, and urban black males in the 1960s may have brought street cool to a level of cultural sophistication, but street swagger in music can be marked from the 1980s, when the aggressive posturing, macho braggadocio, ghetto-articulate, and stylishly dressed performance of black masculinity by Run-DMC transformed inner-city street culture into pop culture. Swagger may refer not only to hardcore rap performers but any powerfully performing male, from the street savvy yet elegant masculine performance of Jay-Z to the coolly restrained and self-assured manner of Barack Obama, who is no stranger to the street. The term is not exclusive to men, however, as I doubt anyone would suggest that Mary J. Blige does not have swagger.

## Reckless Eyeballing:
## The Politics of Facial Performance

Facial expression has also become a critical index of masculine performance, often projected through the intense gaze referred to as *mean mugging*, which has become virtually a cachet with hard styles of rap performance. This gaze, an affect of street attitude, is just as associated with bodily performance as are physical signs and gestures. It also articulates the distance between high and low, the city and the suburb, outsiders and the privileged; it subverts the policing of black bodies and thus may be seen as transgressive. In *The Politics and Poetics of Transgression*, Peter Stallybrass and Allon White argue that, for the English bourgeoisie, the organization of the gaze was always problematic in that the gaze of the Other as a "contaminating touch" could not be controlled, since "even if the bourgeoisie could establish the purity of their own gaze, the stare of the urban poor themselves was rarely felt as one of deference and respect. On the contrary, it was more frequently seen as an aggressive and humiliating act of physical contact."[39] The gangsta/thug gaze signifies upon and critiques relations of race, power, and social position[40] in that the defiant gaze and aggressive physical posturing, for example, the iconic b-boy stance, in much hardcore hip-hop representation become strategies to push back against the Panopticonic gaze of patriarchal structures of power in which black males are made hypervisible and the subject of constant surveillance by institutions of state power and media. Contrarily, such representations resist control while inviting it, as they transform class and racial grievance into performance art. Rap music videos are spaces that make possible the consumption of spectacularized images of black masculinity that are simultaneously evasive and invasive—evasive because the images in these videos resist the control and censure to which black males are subject, and invasive because they negotiate the distance between themselves and those who both fear and desire the racial transgression the images present. In this case, the Panopticonic gaze is turned back on itself by those it has sought to confine.

Mean mugging may be read as recuperative in that it rejects the stereotype of the perennially grinning southern plantation darkie who has little choice but to bend under the weight of white patriarchal oppression. It also rejects feminization and vulnerability through the withholding of emotion but is nonetheless a powerful affective display that telegraphs hypermasculinity and potential aggression. bell hooks (1995b) suggests that white patriarchal objectification of the black male begins with the equation of black men with the body, nature, and the feminine, all of which were subject to control by white males. Black men were "symbolically castrated" after slavery and "constructed as feminine by white supremacist rhetoric" that equated blacks with the feminine, that is, instinctual, helpless, and dependent upon white male patriarchy in order to survive. In resistance to this construction, black males cultivated and embraced the "hypermasculine image"[41] while rejecting the feminine, which undoubtedly has much to do with the misogynistic tone of much hardcore rap. The act of smiling and presenting a pleasing demeanor as part of the onstage performance is thus rejected and empathetically telegraphed through mean mugging in tandem with other aggressive body language such as clenched fists and the so-called b-boy stance—a sideways positioning of the body, arms folded across the chest, and head cocked defiantly to one side—an iconic look mainstreamed by Run-DMC.

In the song "Real Nigga Roll Call," Ice Cube delivers a lyric line that articulates how weak masculine demeanor, including smiling, is held in contempt in hardcore masculine performance, where "real niggas" are fearless, powerful, and authentically black, when he rhymes "See I'ma mean nigga/Youse afraid nigga/Ol' pretend nigga/Smile and grin nigga/I hate a false nigga/Diana Ross nigga." The idea of the "smile and grin nigga" is trumped by a "mean nigga," whose masculinity and sense of self as a powerful social actor are uncompromised. Ice Cube's choice of Ross, whom Berry Gordy chose to promote Motown's crossover market strategy to white audiences in the 1960s, mocks her reputation for disingenuous fawning. The kind of man who is a "Diana Ross nigga" is not only emasculated and feminized but inauthentic and fake. These lyrics also suggest how the hypermasculine can be declared "in words that convey and assert action and domination [and where] verbal humiliation as well as physical prowess" are employed to stress one's hardness, especially in the face of opposition, so that "in the language of black masculinist vernacular, [the 'real' nigga] is the dick fucking the other dude over, turning him into a pussy."[42]

Mean mugging is likely to also take place within the context of any number of physical signifiers or situations that could set the stage for hostilities, and that might include the numerous array of hand signs and signals used in hip-hop culture that constitute a virtual language in themselves, particularly in the social context of gang culture, in which again, they are highly situational and index group affiliation and identity.

## You Got the Look: Urban Street Chic

Relationality, experience, and performance find a wealth of creative expression in the sartorial display of street wear or gear,[43] which plays upon the surface of the body and helps signify social identification and self-identity. For many African Americans, the fetishization of brand-name clothing and an almost competitive sense of fashion trendsetting are long-standing cultural traits that have been no less important in hip-hop culture. Clothing has long been a marker of style for young black male "sports" and night dwellers, indexical of one's socio-cultural background and often telling markers of racial ethnicity and identity. Leon Wynter writes that in junior high school he could tell the race or ethnicity of another boy by looking not at his skin but at his feet. If the boy wore sneakers such as U.S. Keds or an off-label brand the kid was probably white, but if he wore Converse All-Stars he was more likely to be one of the few kids at Frank D. Whelan Junior High in the north Bronx who were African American or one of the tiny handfuls of Puerto Ricans who attended the school. The importance of brand-name sneakers and other designer apparel has become just as indexical in hip-hop culture, if not more so, where fashion choices might indicate one's affiliation with a certain artist, style of music, or geographical location. Adopting black fashion, music, and style has been one way in which white kids indicate the breaking away from mainstream values, since African American fashion, music, and style "were by definition not part of the mainstream, because mainstream meant white. White kids who embraced the markers of nonwhite cultural identity opted out of the mainstream, as defined, and thus out of whiteness itself."[44]

From the days when athletic jerseys from the defunct Negro League baseball teams were in vogue, the reverse-turned baseball cap became part of the iconographic narrative of hip-hop culture, a powerfully innovative fashion statement signaling a coutural revolution to come. Urban street clothing would encompass the stylization of sports footwear and athletic attire, the commodification of the oversized "baggy" look in pants that often leave the underwear visible above the waistband and other looks adopted from black street culture. Hip-hop-derived urban casual attire has generated a billion-dollar fashion industry by translating urbanity and blackness into designer apparel. The sartorial performance surrounding hardcore styles of music in hip-hop culture that gradually became mainstreamed into hip-hop youth culture over the next two decades would reference the black male body as a nexus point for the convergence of inner-city street culture, prison culture, and the culture of sport. Run-DMC had perhaps the most critical impact on the commodification of urban street culture, popularizing oversized, ostentatious gold chains, brand-name sneakers, and other athletic clothing as casual wear. Run-DMC's hip new street aesthetic, a look that included black leather, fedoras, aggressive body posturing, and mean mugging, were fitting visual accompaniment to the dense, loud beats and aggressive vocal delivery of the group's music, all of which moved hip-hop music and culture toward an edgier, harder, macho-centered cultural aesthetic. Run-DMC was "the first group that came onstage as if they had just come off the street corner."[45] This shift in the representation of the black male body in popular music performance would set the stage for a radically new kind of urban theater where the line between the real and performance would gradually become indistinguishable.

The arrival of West Coast gangsta rap in the late 1980s popularized other kinds of looks associated with Los Angeles area street culture into the music, some associated with prison culture such as that of droopy pants produced because the wearing of belts is forbidden in the penal system. Tommy Hilfiger would be one of the first prominent fashion houses to transform urban street wear into haute couture by appropriating its most identifiable markers, including the baggy fit of beltless pants and designer hoodies. With the increasing prominence of commodity branding, the bold display of designer names integrated the aesthetic display of stylized text onto apparel, so that words—the names of the designers—became important in themselves and began to play and signify upon the surface of clothing much as clothing played upon the surface of bodies. It was no longer cachet to merely wear a brand-name designer, but the designer's name or brand must be prominently displayed in self-reflexive move that gave branding an importance out of all proportion in hip-hop couture.

Hip-hop artists and entrepreneurs began to contract lucrative deals for clothing lines—FUBU, Sean Jean, Phat Farm, Shadywear, G-Unit, Roc-A-Wear, and numerous others—that created a highly visible synergy between music and designer fashion in an unprecedented way. Designer names could now index one's choice in music or interest in a particular artist. Baseball caps, sneakers, sports jerseys, and other casual wear would become more exotic and prized as commodity items and markers of cultural hipness, especially as they became tied to major artists and brands. Even the stocking cap, or doo-rag, a headdress used by males that was nothing more than a cut-off leg of women's panty hose, has been updated, stylized, and commodified as an urban fashion accessory that references a street look of masculine toughness. The stocking cap may be more familiar as a face-covering for perpetrators of violent crimes. The stylized doo-rag then, indexes both the urban black male and criminality, and is thus an item of clothing imbued with ominous affective power. The bandana[46] perhaps best illustrates how color becomes a situating factor in clothing and adornment in that the term *colors* in urban street culture typically refers to gang affiliation, for example, blue indicating Crips and red indicating Bloods, the two violent street gang factions that figured prominently in the crack cocaine wars of the 1980s and in the subsequent rise of West Coast gangsta rap music. Hardcore rappers Ice-T and Snoop Dogg have prominently used the color blue in clothing used for album cover shots, a fact that seems inconsequential unless one knows that both rappers have professed association with Los Angeles area Crips sets.

## Making Beats, Making Rhymes

Rap's musical language—its beats—signifies upon, challenges, subverts, and deconstructs Western notions of music, musician, and musicality that may be read as oppositional socio-political texts, primal screams of existential discontent from the marginalized and maligned who refuse to go quietly into the dark night of the American Dream, but which do not sacrifice play and pleasure on the road to sonic dissension. The poetics of rap, on the other hand—its rhymes—have been just as provocative in their subversion of language, including the deliberate use of incendiary words that have unfortunately detracted from what has been in many cases accomplished poetry dedicated to the power and possibility of language that rivals European poetic traditions.

With respect to the musical side of this process, the African diasporic reference to the drum that the term *beats* implies engages ages-old African ideals of sound aesthetics while the new technologies of sound situate it in the contemporary world through strategies of fragmentation, disruption, discontinuity, and ahistoricity. As Tricia Rose remarks in her seminal book *Black Noise*, "rap's musical elements and its use of music technology are a crucial aspect of the development of the form and are absolutely critical to the evolution of hip-hop generally"[47] in establishing a "postindustrial urban context" for black youth music. Rap's rhythms, its most perceptive yet least material elements, are its most powerful affective component, defining the music as a primarily sonic cultural phenomenon that is part of the history of diasporic African American music making in the New World even as it purports to be something radically different through the uses of technology and the fact of social rupture in the contemporary postindustrial city at the turn of the century. The mapping of sophisticated rhythms onto indeterminately pitched sound recuperates the African aesthetic of "found" sound that operates in what Olly Wilson has characterized as "the heterogeneous sound ideal" in African American music, and that privileges "musical events in which rhythmic clash or disagreement of accents is the ideal, and cross-rhythm and metrical ambiguity are the accepted, expected norm." This ideal of sound not only tends to fill up musical space but also attempts to "incorporate physical body motion as an integral part of the music making process."[48] Rhymes and beats are often not fully distinguished as separate but equally important aspects of hip-hop music, each with its own strategies and methods for evoking emotional response. Sound is always more immediate, more profoundly evocative. It produces emotional response in the absence of a linguistic language.

In *Philosophy in a New Key,* Susanne Langer examines the affective power of music as a way to make a distinction between content and form and to focus on "the *emotional* response it is commonly supposed to evoke" and that can be appreciated regardless of music's particular structural components.[49] What music does is to deal in the morphology of feeling, using tensions and resolutions associated with tonal relationships to evoke feelings that are not quite emotions and not quite ideas. Music is nonverbal and symbolic, the "formulation and representation of emotions, moods, mental tensions and resolution"[50] that speaks in the language of the figurative rather than the literal. Beats in hip-hop music, then, are constructed to speak to a range of complex and often conflicted feelings—alienation, despair, hopelessness, rage, joy, opposition, anger, and nihilism—that is the soundtrack to the narratives painted in rhymes and performed through verbal narrative and body-ism. The idea of *tone* at play in hip-hop music must be seen as dealing with the musical parameters of that term and with its nonmusical aspects, so that in addition to pitch and timbre, the music is speaking on other levels, articulating and evoking affective responses that language cannot.

The way in which beats are constructed and in which sound is deployed are as critical in defining what is "hard" and "hardcore" in rap performance as are other elements such as the lyrical language of rhymes, narrative drama, styles of flow, kinds of visual representation, references to space and place, and the performance of masculinity on the body. The use of drum machine samples, loops, and electronic beats began to enter the hip-hop soundscape through old school numbers by Afrika Bambaataa, notably his 1982 releases "Planet Rock" and "Looking for the Perfect Beat" and 1983's *Renegades of Funk.* The songs privileged volume and the insistent crack and boom of the Roland TR 808, creating the soundscape of electronic techno-funk. It was the sound of the urban street and of a new sensibility rising from the black ghetto just as Run-DMC would begin its ascendency and crack cocaine began to hit the streets. The tone of the early old school music, however, spoke not to nihilistic despair but to joy, hope, and a vision of social unity that still largely defines and informs the "alternative" in hip-hop, which puts it some-what outside the scope of much rap music in the commercial marketplace. Afrika Bambaataa, like Duke Ellington, painted new landscapes of sound and meaning using the dissonances and abrasions of urban modernity and the black vernacular expressed through music that spoke to the contemporary black experience as well as to history. Like Ellington, Bambaataa embraced the past and acknowledged the present, creating a new musical template for the future that would redefine the way in which black music and culture was represented to and in the world.

Coming out just months after "Planet Rock," Grandmaster Flash and the Furious Five's 1982 single "The Message," rapped by Melle Mel, changed the tone of Bambaataa's Zulu Nation–inspired utopia by reinserting a desper-ate realism in the music that reasserted some of the dimmer realities of the postindustrial city. "The Message" announced the end of hip-hop's old school house party and the future of hip-hop, which slowly began to embrace real-ism, the urban street, and address the marginalization of inner-city black youth. It would be the realism of the street that would prevail by the middle of the next decade, moving a harder style of rap performance and its accom-panying aesthetic of the ghetto to the very center of mainstream American popular music. Run-DMC's 1983 releases "It's Like That" and "Sucka MCs" introduced hip-hop's new school in sound and representation, synthesizing the idea of hard beats (using electronic drum machine loops and a sparse, stripped-down sound), the idea of hard masculinity through aggressive body-ism, and the violence that began to invade the urban street in the epidemic of crack cocaine and the drug wars. Run-DMC would privilege a new aesthetic and a new attitude where volume became sonic aggression and social protest, while the use of multi-tracking, of piling tracks on top of each other to create dense sonic textures was the hallmark of Public Enemy's production team.

The studio aesthetic of "working in the red"[51] to produce music that was not only loud, but distorted and dissonant, would become the sonic equivalent to Public Enemy's righteous indignation and later, to N.W.A.'s intemperate nihilism. The music's sonic ruptures and fragmented, decentered soundscapes pointed the way toward new representations of music, race, and gender that had social as well as political implications. The music's enveloping and dis-tinctive bass-heavy sound "does not rest outside of its musical and social power [since] emotional power and presence in rap are profoundly linked to sonic force and one's receptivity to it."[52] This new aesthetic of sound in hip-hop music—low-frequency, high-volume sounds that crackled, hissed, hummed, and boomed, a multitude of electronic samples, loops, and driving repetitive rhythms—would be defined, refined, and edged from the hard to the hardcore by a handful of new school rap artists who released seminal records within a relatively short time span from 1983 to 1988. "Sucka MC's" made little attempt at melody or harmony, replicating instead old school style braggadocio, macho posturing, and boasting. Nonetheless, staccato-styled vocal flow against the cavernous sound of synthesized cracks and kicks was a cacophonous beat down delivered with bombast and attitude. "It's Like That" and "Sucka MC's" set a new tone and standard for sound production and street-wise masculine bravado that defined the full scope of the hard aesthetic that others would soon emulate and eclipse.

The rapper LL Cool J followed Run-DMC's lead and style in 1984 with "I Need a Beat," a song that sounded strikingly similar in many respects to "Sucka MC's"—hard drum machine-like minimalism and a flow that bobbed, weaved, and threw uppercuts at the microphone. Although on different labels (Run-DMC on Profile and LL on the newly formed Def Jam) the two acts shared a connection in that Def Jam co-founder Russell Simmons was brother to Run-DMC's Joseph "Run" Simmons, which may have had something to do with the resemblance in the production styles of the two songs. LL Cool J's 1987 "I'm Bad" is memorable if only because the song's opening sequence samples a police siren and the scratchy voice of a police dispatcher alerting cruisers to be on the lookout for a black male fugitive, setting up a chase scene out of the 1971 film *Sweet Sweetback's Baadasssss Song*. The scenario of black men in a police confrontation had already been enacted at the end of "The Message," itself an adaptation of a police drug arrest that occurs at the end of Stevie Wonder's 1973 song "Living for the City." All three scenarios complicate black inner-city males and their relationship with the postindustrial urban city and the police, particularly since the 1960s. LL Cool J edged toward (re)representing the stereotype of the black male as urban brute and antiheroic street thug, a theme that was extended by Philadelphia rapper Schoolly D, who was also busy reinventing the urban black male rap persona with a sound of his own.

## Hustlers of Flow: The Art of Verbal Performance

With Run-DMC, Public Enemy, LL Cool J, and numerous other contemporary pioneers of hip-hop's verbal performance, new school rhymes became more artfully constructed, more complexly crafted, and more serious in tone as well as more infinitely diverse. Whereas old school rhymes might go on in endless streams of associations or in simple rhymed couplets, newer artists began to weave internal rhyming schemes into narratives that told complexly layered stories loaded with coded street slang and virtually indecipherable puns. The construction of rhymes and their vocal delivery comprise any rapper's unique verbal flow, as individual in terms of style as the signature sound of a well-known jazz performer. The variety and styles of flow, although highly individualistic, nonetheless have progenitors, those who have shown others the way in the same manner that Louis Armstrong and Charlie Parker influenced virtually every jazz musician who came after them. The art of flow goes to the heart of the rap performer as performing artist and is a subject whose breadth and scope I cannot hope to adequately cover here. Nonetheless, I will make a number of broad observations to suggest how it fits into the mediascape I have posed.

One of the first truly original masters of flow, as important to the development of contemporary rapping styles as Grandmaster Flash was to the evolution of the modern DJ, is William "Rakim" Griffin, who performed with DJ Eric Barrier under the name Eric B and Rakim. Rakim did not invent flow, but he certainly revolutionized it on record. The style he introduced on the 1987 album *Paid in Full* (with strong follow-ups on 1988's *Follow the Leader* and 1990s *Let the Rhythm Hit 'Em*) was precise, well-crafted, adroit, and highly rhythmic, a rapid-fire high wire act that was as athletic as a B-Boy's latest spin move, with a logic to its internal rhymes that every great rap artist after him would adopt. What Rakim brought to the art was nothing less than a sense of what could be done with rap if the wordplay was taken seriously as craft and high art. Rakim's delivery was as fresh as freestyle, with verses dense in metaphor and vivid imagery that were innovative and visionary. Rakim opens "Follow the Leader" with the rhyme "Follow me into a solo/ Get in the flow/And you could pitch it like a photo," which not only rhymes the words *solo* and *flow* with *photo*, but self-reflexively calls attention to the verse as it unravels itself. A few lines later he quadruples up his rhymes in the verse "The *Supreme* before a microphone, still I *fiend*/This was a *tape* I wasn't supposed to *break*/I was supposed to *wait*, but let's *motivate*." Proclaiming himself supreme on the microphone, he is nonetheless addicted to the performance, unable to hold himself back, but needing to break out on a lyrical flow during what may have just been a practice run because he is so highly motivated. On "Let the Rhythm Hit 'Em," one of his signature performances, his words become weapons when he rhymes "I'm the arsenal, I got *artillery*, lyrics of *ammo*/ rounds of *rhythm*, then I'm a give 'em *piano*/ Bring a bullet-proof *vest*/nothin' to *ricochet*." Rakim's use of figurative language constructs lines of lyrical violence as aesthetic warfare, juxtaposing the art of rhyme with the tools of crime. His "stream of consciousness"-styled flow is saturated with syncopated rhythms as sophisticated as those of a jazz performer; the self-reflexive boasts of lyrical prowess and mastery over his opponents takes poetic imagery to the street as a rowdy rumble. Rakim brought the vibe of battle rapping to vinyl; within the animated sound arena that Eric B. constructed around him, Rakim mastered the sweet science of the pugilistic beat down as a combination of verbal style, wit, and swagger.

Rakim's flow was very different from that of new school innovators Run-DMC, whose lines were often simply constructed in old school-style rhymed couplets ("People in the world try to make ends meet/You try to ride car, train, bus or feet") but whose power lay in the way they were spit (spoken) into the microphone—aggressive, heavily punctuated, hard down on the beat, and intensely rendered in terms of volume and tone. Rakim was more suave. He laid back and cruised, rhyming ahead of the beat, on top of it, and around it, orbiting it like a moon, his flow defying the gravity of Eric's cacophonous tracks. Arguably, many rap performers that followed them largely took one path or the other—the muscular, militant, almost pummeling style of Run-DMC, or the nimble, dexterous 'blink and you missed it' wordplay of Rakim, a kind of flow that whispered braggadocio in your ear rather than shouted it in your face.

The pantheon of innovative performers who have helped move the art forward include certainly performers such as Big Daddy Kane, Biz Markie, Kurtis Blow, De La Soul, Digital Underground, Ice Cube (with and without N.W.A), Ice-T, Kool Moe Dee, LL Cool J, Public Enemy, Snoop Dogg, Schoolly D, Slick Rick, Biggie Smalls, Tupac Shakur, Eminem, and Jay-Z. Trying to name each, and what they brought to the table, would be like trying to name every innovative jazz musician and the particular way each moved the art forward just another step, but each of these and many more brought something different to rhyming that was emulated by those that came next, although the idea of "biting" the style of another rapper is not necessarily seen as a form of regard and respect as it often is in jazz.

In terms of contemporary performance, however, the flow and the meta-narrative of hardcore hip-hop begins to change with three performers who arguably stand out from the rest: Snoop Dogg, Tupac Shakur, and Biggie Smalls. All three introduced elements of gang and/or drug culture into the language of rap in such a way that the subtext of violence that lay beneath the surface was barely noticed, or was simply unable to be deciphered, or was so lost in hypnotic dance beats that no one cared anyway. They also introduced narratives providing autobiographical details of their own lives that were deeply personal, and styles of flow that were conversational, accessible, and helped move them as performers of hardcore rap beyond the one-dimensional characters that litter the genre. Their narratives and personal dramas spoke to broader themes of human struggle against often unfair and unreasonable odds (interspersed with plenty of party anthems), thus complicating their own life stories for others, which added to the universal appeal of all three. Still, they are all quite different as masters of flow. Snoop Dogg's laconic chronic-drenched drawl invited everybody into a house party, gin and juice all around, really introducing a new kind of listener-friendly style that did not alienate the listener even as he told nefarious tales. Biggie replicated that kind of flow on the East Coast, and to some extent so did Tupac; they talked *to* the listeners instead of *at* them, and this was another kind of revolution in the art of flow. By combining artfully complex internal rhymes with the drama of their own lives—providing an experiential quality of universality that seemed to resonate with larger audiences—this served to humanize otherwise brutish public personas, broadening their appeal and mainstreaming the genre. They became wise hoodlums, urban contemporary versions perhaps of the noble savage, but they sold records across boundaries of class, gender, race, and nationality.

What is best in these three performers would converge and be magnified in the style and artistry of Jay-Z, whom I discuss at length in the following chapter. In reflecting on the evolution of rap's poetics, Jay-Z, ever the adept observer, gets it right in commenting that the best rappers "from the earliest days distinguished themselves by looking closely at the world around them and describing it in a clever, artful way. And then they went further than just describing it. They started commenting on it in a critical way"[53] that becomes great social commentary, and often great art. Jay-Z's lyrics certainly embody his own observations, perhaps summed up best in a verse from his song "Renegade" from his 2001 album *The Blueprint*: "My childhood didn't mean much, only raising green up/Raising my fingers to critics, raising my head to the sky/BIG I did it—multi before I die, nigga/No lie, just know I chose my own fate/I drove by the fork in the road and went straight." Through the use of internal rhymes and metaphor, he sums up his whole life—his trajectory from a teenage drug dealer to a multimillionaire who was eventually able to find an honest path—in a few compressed lines. He also eloquently sums up the irony and contradiction of young black males like himself who are forced to make what he considers a "false choice between poverty and breaking the law." He expresses defiance ("raising my fingers to critics") to those who judge him for having to choose an illegal way of making money ("raising green up") while trying to keep his dignity and humanity intact ("raising my head to the sky") and turning for salvation to his love of music, the thing that eventually allowed him to come to a critical juncture in his life where he had a real choice, to continue in a violently criminal lifestyle or go straight and live within the law. He chose the latter.

Perhaps no song in rap demonstrates how two styles of flow can be so diametrically opposed to each other than "Renegade," which also features rhymes by Eminem. Jay-Z, unlike many rap artists, has constantly shown off different methodologies of flow over his long career, altering the cadence, delivery, tone, and verbal nuances of his style in order, as he would have it, to keep others from copying him. He can affect the speed and dexterity of Buster Rhymes and Big Daddy Kane or the serpentine wit of Tupac and Biggie. On "Renegade," his flow is deliberately unorthodox and angular, while Eminem spits composed, precisely metered rhymes in off-beat, accented sixteen-note figures that use a series of measured internal rhyme schemes, as in the opening lines: "Since I'm in a position to talk to these kids and they listen/I ain't no politician but I'll kick it with 'em a minute/Cause see they call me a menace, and if the shoe fits I'll wear it/But if it don't, then y'all can swallow the truth grin and bear it." Many consider this track one of the best rhymes of Eminem's career, a defiant attack on his own critics told with an impeccably timed rhythmic flow and musicality that demonstrates a mastery of the form. It is a grand performance that even Jay-Z acknowledges on "A Star is Born" from 2009's *The Blueprint 3* album. Jay-Z and Eminem could not be more radically different from each other in terms of tone, content, and personal narrative. They have staked out very different approaches to the performance of masculinity, but their very different styles of vocal delivery, as personal as fingerprints, set them apart as much as narrative content, the dramatic elements they play out, and their individual personal histories. It is all of these things together, with each informing the other, that help shape a particular hip-hop artist's persona and that attracts followings, but none of it works without the ability to spit a rhyme with skill and imagination. Beats and narrative content almost always matter, but the art of flow has its own sublime aesthetic. [54]

## Fighting Words: Provocateurs of the Vernacular

Regardless of the toning down of language in much commercial mainstream rap since the 1990s, words continue to define the hardcore in hip-hop's musical dialectic of beat making and rhyming, meaning that words can be realized in ways that situate rap performance as either hard, hardcore, or what is now lumped into the category of alternative styles. Language, then, both the choice of certain words and the content of the narratives these words weave, determines the *tone* of the music in terms of defining its character. The term *alternative* suggests a usage similar to that of rock music to designate something that exists outside the popular and commercial center, but there seems to be less distinction between much contemporary rock music other than what may be regarded as generational; it is much more stylistically diverse, but the Beatles were more eclectic than much of what now passes for alternative rock. In hip-hop, distinctions are considerably more stark between music that is considered mainstream commercial (this encompasses most hardcore styles of rap) and seen as having dubious social merit, and that which aspires to some higher moral or socially redemptive purpose. It is often a fine line. Nonetheless, it is largely language that provides the basis for deciding what is and is not hardcore in contemporary rap music performance, either because they broach certain subject matter deemed offensive to some public code of morality or decency, or because the material is considered "adult" and therefore subject to regulation in much the same way that some movies and television shows are prohibited for younger audiences. This continues to be a fairly gray area in many cases. The provocative language and subject matter deployed in hardcore styles of rap performance define it as graphic because of extreme violence, or explicit sexual content, or instances of profanity. The latter has become much less of an issue since explicit language can now easily be bleeped out. It is now common practice given the popularity of the genre for certain artists to release explicit and bowdlerized versions of the same song for family-oriented retail outlets or for platforms such as Apple's iTunes music store, which often offers both versions.

These commercial compromises suggest the importance placed on language, on the use of particular words seen as incendiary, obscene, profane, salacious, violent, or socially repugnant in some way. Such views, however, are relational to any number of social, historical, and/or cultural contexts. The ways that words are intentionally and strategically used to produce powerfully affective responses have been relatively overlooked in much of the critical commentary on rap, which is to say that the affective nature of language itself in hardcore performance deserves a closer look. The inclusion of words like *bitch* or *nigga* and other provocative language are critical elements that move hip-hop performance into the realm of hardcore. To dismiss the study of music that contains such language outright is to negate a fuller investigation not only of the music but of language, audience, and reception, which is to suggest that responses to certain kinds of language must at least be seen as highly situational. Postwar linguistics and its focus on the theoretical, abstract, and, thus, cognitive nature of language has largely ignored non-cognitive side aspects of language such as the "objectification of emotional experience" in which language regenerates its emotional power through artistic expression.[55] This has certainly been true of the African American engagement with the English language over the course of American history, hip-hop being only the most recent example in an array of performance practices that have regenerated the vernacular use of language while reinvigorating black expressive forms.

African American popular music has always employed the vernacular of the disadvantaged and dispossessed. As a large segment of African American culture has become more educated and literate, one could certainly argue that it has distanced itself from traditional avenues of black oral and musical expressivity, and thus from a powerful aspect of black cultural heritage. The invigoration of the emotive and expressive in language has typically found renewal and (re)invention in the black working class as with the formation of blues, spirituals, jazz, spoken word poetry, and other vernacular black expressive forms. In the case of contemporary hip-hop, language tends to be personally liberatory as well as culturally recuperative, speaking to issues of self-identity and marginalization within the working class as well as the black underclass, those who are the most disadvantaged and dispossessed with the fewest life chances.[56] Hardcore rap typically contains both graphic themes and extreme profanity that performers deploy fully aware of their incendiary and provocative power to elicit outraged responses from those outside this culture.[57]

Nonetheless, merely suppressive responses to provocative language and themes used in hardcore rap that tend to limit further inquiry only result in forms of censorship that accomplish little but to perhaps negate the opportunity for objective inquiries that interrogate how race, class, gender, and other social factors influence how we think about certain words and how we are likely to respond to them and in what contexts. The emergence of hardcore rap and its use of obscenely profane language initiated a debate over graphic and profane words and their presence in the public domain, with race, class, guns, violence, crime, drugs, and misogyny now central to the discourse. The fact that some of the most intemperate and vulgar language to appear in mainstream popular music was a product of street gang–associated, drug-dealing black males from urban ghettos—the apparatus within which hardcore styles of rap is constructed—was both alarming to middle-class whites and embarrassing to middle-class blacks. Reactions to hardcore rap performers in the late 1980s tended, however, to dismiss the historical prevalence of off-color language in black vernacular expressive art forms. Hardcore rap music may be viewed in the same way that "race records" were in the early decades of the twentieth century, which is to say they were made by and for a largely black listening audience. Much postwar rhythm and blues was similarly produced and consumed. It was not until rhythm and blues began to cross racial lines that its more suggestive subtexts were closely scrutinized, causing any number of rhythm and blues songs to be banned from radio playlists after the ascent of rock 'n' roll. The rock 'n' roll that was allowed to be promoted to white teens and played on the public airwaves was necessarily bowdlerized of much of its salty language.

The public debate around issues of language use in hardcore rap conveniently obfuscated broader issues such as the desperate economic and social status of black inner-city youth for whom incendiary language was, as some of them quickly perceived, a way to gain notoriety and sell records. The controversy did not diminish the use of graphic language in hip-hop but in fact had quite the opposite effect. On the other hand, much of the language that these records contained more or less reflected its use among the producers of this particular music and to a large segment of their audience for whom such words may fall within the range of the language they use in daily communication, which is to say that hardcore rap music most often employs the vernacular language of the black urban street from which it comes. The fact that it has tremendous emotive power is what gives it a ground of authenticity and legitimacy for many, even though it contains themes and expletives that may not be used in polite company. This is certainly true of a variety of black expressive cultural forms. African American oral epic poems known as "toasts" or "pimp narratives" are rich with this kind of language and humor though it is no longer exclusive to the culture of pimps, hustlers, ex-convicts, and street poets who have helped to perpetuate them.[58] They are certainly known to many hardcore rappers but they can be found in black culture whether in the North or the South and points in between since these kinds of oral heroic epics can be traced back at least to Reconstruction.

Comedian Rudy Ray Moore may have been the most preeminent user of pimp narratives in his party records, recordings of profane humor made by stand-up comedians such as Moore, Moms Mabley, Jimmy Lynch, Redd Foxx, and numerous others that were largely confined to black audiences at private gatherings or nightclubs until Richard Pryor crossed over into the popular mainstream after the release of his live recording *That Nigger's Crazy* in 1974, making him a household name among many blacks and whites as well. Profanity-laced hardcore songs arguably owe a debt to the toasting tradition, which may account for some of the boasting and misogynistic language. Many West Coast hardcore rappers in particular, such as Snoop Dogg and Ice-T, who have lived the life of street hustling, pimping, and incarceration, are well aware of this tradition and the work of Moore, whose Dolemite character enjoys legendary status among many black males. It is this tradition of vernacular language use that Henry Louis Gates Jr. felt deserved defending in the legal battle over free speech and obscenity that surrounded the rap group 2 Live Crew and its 1989 album *As Nasty As They Wanna Be.* Coming to his own defense in a 1990 article in *The New York Times*, Gates poses the question of whether or not the obscenity charges brought against the group might be related "to the specter of the young black male as a figure of sexual and social disruption, the very stereotypes 2 Live Crew seems determined to undermine."[59] Gates' suggestion that 2 Live Crew was all about undermining sexual stereotypes may be a little disingenuous, as if "Me So Horny" really had some deeper moral point to make. Nonetheless, Gates' testimony underscored two points worth mentioning. The first is that black working-class vernacular language has historically been more tolerant of words that others might find objectionable, and that 2 Live Crew's music would probably not have been of such interest to Broward County authorities in Florida if it had only circulated within black communities, which was largely true of black party records until Richard Pryor. The second point is that objectionable language, whether explicitly sexual or violent, has tended to provoke stronger affective responses when coming from young black males.[60] The way that rap-related offenses such as vulgar language and scenarios of violence are discussed in popular media, writes Tricia Rose, "is fundamentally linked to the larger social discourse on the spatial control of black people,"[61] but also exposes the very real tensions and fissures between white (and even black middle-class) mores and expressions of black folk vernacular that go beyond the pale.

## Situation Critical: The Drama of Lived Experience

Schoolly D took the metaphors of hardness introduced by Run-DMC and added street gang realism and explicit narratives of sex, drugs, and casual violence. Schoolly D's music would again irrevocably change the tone of hip-hop's musical sound by setting the template for what would become the hardcore aesthetic in rap performance with songs like "Gangster Boogie/ Maniac," "CIA/Cold Blooded Blitz," and "Saturday Night." The 1987 single "P.S.K. What Does it Mean?" in particular, from the *Saturday Night* album, established him as a pioneer of hardcore, assisted by DJ Code Money's backing track, punctuated by rapid beats made to sound like machine gun fire and a kick drum that hauled off shotgun booms. The combination of sound and lyrical content took the music in a new direction that others began to imitate, bringing the new realities of the urban street into hip-hop's core narrative.

The experiential aspect of this intrusion—the participation of gang members and drug dealers in what had until then been a largely benign music— and the effect of offensive rhetoric, lyrics, and narratives as situational in recontextualizing this music cannot be overstated. Even given the tolerance for objectionable language and themes in vernacular traditions, the graphic language and horrific mayhem that arose from inner-city street gang culture and permeated hip-hop culture during the 1980s was without precedent in black popular music and culture. The fact that hardcore gangsta rap reflected a number of inconvenient truths—the desperation that existed in urban ghettos, the plague of crack cocaine, and gun violence—that it gave name to actual geographical locations, that it exposed a demographic that had been written off by society and was now pissed off and acting out only served to demonize young black males who were both victims and predators as 1960s' rage and frustration became 1980s' hopelessness and nihilism. Schoolly D appears to be the first to use references to gangs and drugs, misogynistic themes, images of gunplay and casual violence, and the word *nigga* as the contextual matrix. Run-DMC may have defined "hardness" in rap music and masculine performance, but it was Schoolly D who defined the "hardcore" through words and narrative content constructed in the register of the real.

Within a year of Schoolly D's assent, South Bronx–based Boogie Down Productions, featuring KRS-ONE and the late Scott La Rock, released "9mm Goes Bang" on the 1987 album *Criminal Minded*. The single may be the first rap song to use the term *crack dealer* in its narrative ("I knew a crack dealer his name was Peter/had to buck him down with my 9mm") and to depict scenarios of drug dealing and retaliatory gang violence told through the song's protagonist, a drug dealer who executes three gang members in a violent shootout that was, again, something new and disturbing in black popular music. The relationship between the crack game and the rap game became indelibly linked over the next two decades as the terms *gangbanger* and *drive-by* entered the American lexicon during the crack cocaine wars of the 1980s.[62]

Early hip-hop lyricism was in fact quite G-rated, but the language of violence and the reality of street-level drug dealing provided an unlimited range of narrative possibilities for those straddling the worlds of hip-hop culture and street gang culture. The cover of *Criminal Minded* appears to be the first in hip-hop to privilege the iconography of the gun as it features a photo of group members KRS-ONE and Scott La Rock wearing ammunition belts and brandishing weapons. The shift to more profane and obscene language, explicit sexual content, graphic depictions of casual violence, drugs, and representations of urban masculinity all helped to signal the sea change from the hard to the hardcore in hip-hop culture and rap music. The use of profane language containing pornographic and misogynistic content and narratives of gangbanging and drug dealing would become the defining features of hardcore beginning in the mid-1980s as hip-hop culture, street gang culture, and the epidemic of crack cocaine collided.

Hip-hop would take an even darker turn into violence and realism with West Coast rapper Ice-T's "6 in the Morning," released as a single in 1986 and on the 1987 album *Rhyme Pays*. The song transverses a day in the life of a street hustler and depicts horrific scenes of misogynistic violence as well as a shootout with police. On this and later records Ice-T extended narrative themes explored by Boogie Down Productions and Schoolly D ("6 in the Morning" was based in part on Schoolly D's "P.S.K. What Does It Mean?") as well as gun iconography on his 1988 album *Power*, which features group members wielding shotguns and an Uzi automatic pistol. N.W.A.'s 1988 album *Straight Outta Compton* again changed the tone of hip-hop music and culture (and continued the idea of using gun imagery on its cover, in this case, the view from a person on the street about to be executed) by essentially turning up the volume on everything that its predecessors had let out in the open, depicting drive-by shootings, drug use, casual violence, and gratuitous misogyny. It was also a better produced record than anything that had come out of a hip-hop studio up to that point. The rough-neck rawness of Run-DMC and the sonic beat-down of Schoolly D were reorchestrated by Dr. Dre into a cleaner, more sophisticated textural density and intensity, producing an album that was as smart as it was vulgar. It demonstrated a mastery of studio production techniques such as sampling, looping, multi-tracking, and low-frequency drum machine booms that became a staple of West Coast hardcore. The record's best songs—"Gangsta Gangsta," "Straight Outta Compton," and "Fuck Tha Police"—as offensive as they might have been, were nonetheless club-banging dance numbers, a fact that may have been overlooked by critics trying to understand its enormous popularity among black youth. Black popular music has always been music for dancing, so while *Straight Outta Compton* may have been the backdrop for violence-laden depictions of Southern California street gang life, it was also a dance floor throw-down that was hard to resist.

Dr. Dre redefined the sound of West Coast hardcore again with his even more technically accomplished 1992 album *The Chronic*, introducing bass-heavy, digitally sampled Parliament-Funkadelic bass and synthesizer sounds and slower, laid-back, but still danceable tempos. The record's lyrical vocal flows, less aggressive and overtly violent, helped establish a beachhead for hardcore rap in the popular mainstream. In many respects, the success of *The Chronic* meant the death of the style of gangsta rap that Dre had helped to define, and he has said as much. Radio and the new culture of video had little tolerance for the raw sound and language of the inner city or the angry young black males who represented it. Hardcore styles, leavened and made less militant, would have never crossed over to a larger audience had it not transfigured into something more palatable for the marketplace. Dr.

Dre pointed the music in a compromise direction that kept much of its street-oriented content but toned down the aggressive beats and much of the vitriol in what might be tagged "gangsta lite." It was a formula that made possible the next wave of hardcore performance—Notorious B.I.G., Tupac, and others who gave rise to East Coast "thug rap," which retained violent and drug-laden themes with sing-along choruses minus the gang warfare and much of the misogyny. This was finally the formula that allowed hardcore rap to bumrush and transform American music, a transformation that also saw young black males take on iconic new imagery in popular culture where they were polarized between desire and demonization.

Legal scholar Richard Thompson Ford, who writes insightfully on race and racism in society in *The Race Card*, suggests that it is poor blacks who are likely to suffer social backlash from the popularization of hip-hop music and its language and mannerisms of the street. As he points out, while middle-class blacks have more or less appropriated the idioms, inflections, and usage of standardized English, "some ghetto blacks have developed a slang so unique it is almost incomprehensible to outsiders."[63] As if that was not problematic enough, as "ghetto slang diverges more and more from mainstream English, it becomes a powerful symbol of socially undesirable behavior."[64] Such language, then, becomes a way to index the same kind of social attitude, behaviors, and performance of ubermasculine hardness that can be transmitted through the gaze, body posture, or bodily adornment. The popularization of ghetto discourse that has become the defining feature of hardcore styles of music may have few consequences for black performers whose nouveau riche class status allows them to live to some degree beyond race. The same cannot be said for inner-city black youth who have internalized the norms and mannerisms associated with the underclass and that affect their future life chances simply because "store clerks, car dealers, bankers, and employers alike inevitably consider grooming, poise, and demeanor as useful if rough proxies for traits like diligence, integrity, and commitment."[65]

This is not simply a matter of racism, Ford suggests, but does involve a host of factors consequent to racism's legacy in the inner city such that urban black youth may have more difficulty acquiring what sociologist William Julius Wilson calls the *soft* skills that educated, middle-class professionals use to assess how well a person is socialized according to mainstream norms, and which are closely tied to culture as well as to class. As Ford argues, "the affectations and mannerisms of the ghetto poor," which have now, "unfortunately, been defined as *black* culture," are not only seen as intrinsically inferior, but "ghetto traits have come to symbolize anti-social behavior,"[66] a symbolic association that has been greatly enhanced over the last quarter century by hardcore hip-hop music and culture, where the performance of the body figures so prominently. The performing body in hardcore hip-hop and its expression through movement and adornment, musical beats, and words that weave the narratives that it engages and the spaces that surround it suggests how all these elements are *situational* and *relational* to each other and are grounded more or less in both individual and group experience of people who share similar backgrounds of race and class. The creators of this musical culture have transformed experience into an artifice of art with great affective and emotive power using the tools of their everyday lives to construct deep structures of meaning and feeling, as well as consequence.

There is often little separation between the trauma of lived experience that often goes with blackness, impoverishment, and social marginality in the United States, particularly in the lives of young black males who gravitated to the allure and deceit of the streets. It was not really until Melle Mel delivered the street sermon in "The Message" that the dramatic aspect of these experiences was given voice in hip-hop and went on to form the driving meta-narrative of the art for the remainder of the twentieth century. The convergence of street gang culture (and its associations with penal/prison culture), drug culture, and hip-hop culture would add another defining narrative to the drama of hip-hop, and I explore these more in chapter four. It is important here, however, to underscore the relationship between personal and group life experience, and the untenable circumstances and choices presented to young black males in the 1980s with the introduction of crack cocaine into inner-city neighborhoods and the evils that accompanied it. This intrusion added a new dramatic arc to the hip-hop story that essentially began in Philadelphia and moved to New York before it exploded on the West Coast, only to return to the music's roots in New York with detours through the Dirty South and other major urban areas. Rap and masculine performance began to move in tandem with a dark new reality on the street that has been very contradictory in the sense that it has created untold wealth and left a great deal of devastation in its wake during a time in which the country also took a hard turn to the political right. Some rode the wave to higher ground, others got caught in the undertow. In either case, whether the songs that evolved from these transformations celebrated ghetto fabulous riches or recounted the cost in human carnage from alleyways where crack vials traded from one desperate hand to another, they told truths that contradicted and contested quaint notions of an American innocence some would like to believe was only lost on 9/11. The songs that began to flourish in hip-hop in the 1980s told the story of an ugly chapter in American history that many even now would like to dismiss or deny. They also bounced a new generation of heroes up the pop charts and changed the direction of hip-hop forever.

# 4. Real Niggas
## Black Men, Hard Men, and the Rise of Gangsta Culture

The first time I recall hearing gangsta rap was in 1988, in the dormitory room of a private, predominantly white liberal arts college in the Southwest where I was belatedly earning my bachelor's degree in English literature. N.W.A.'s album *Straight Outta Compton* had recently dropped, and a small group of male students whom I knew fairly well were gathered around a CD player giving it the kind of attention one would give a highly anticipated sporting event. I had found my way into the room by following the sound of some seriously funkified music that reminded me of old school bands from back in the day. These kids, all privileged upper-middle-class white students in their late teens who came from safe suburban neighborhoods, were listening to N.W.A.'s "Fuck Tha Police," which sounded to me like a street riot with machine gun fire. I had never heard of the group, or for that matter gangsta rap, but then neither had most of these kids, except for the one who had brought the CD. The language and scenarios filling the room rendered me speechless. It was not that I had not heard this kind of language on records before, littered with the words *nigger*, *motherfucker*, and *bitch*, but only on comedic party records, and never in the presence of whites. The kind of language I was listening to was the black working-class folk vernacular I grew up hearing in night clubs, juke joints, house parties, and other places where black folk congregated, partied, and talked trash to each other. I was not the only person in the room who was speechless at what I was hearing, but the nature of our various silences could not have been more different. I was probably visibly unnerved by the violence, the graphic depictions of "cops dying in L.A.," and the enraged voices of some seriously pissed off black men seemingly running amok. These kids, all much younger than me but who all knew me as the resident assistant in the dormitory, looked up at me vacant-eyed but said nothing, going back to the music, totally entranced. No one seemed chagrined even a little by the fact that a black man had just entered the room in the middle of the racial mayhem unfolding in our midst. I was of no consequence. The real niggas were jumping out of the loudspeakers.

The underground success of N.W.A. and *Straight Outta Compton* set in motion a sea of change in American popular music and culture, and I was unwittingly watching it unfold in its nascent stages—white adolescent males fascinated by young black men weaving narratives of ghetto violence and shootouts with cops told in the most graphic of language. Its tone, use of language, and delivery of vocal rhymes was like nothing I had heard before, at least not as music. *Straight Outta Compton* flipped hip-hop music on its head and began the bumrushing of the American pop music mainstream, the aftershocks of which would exile political and socially conscious styles of hip-hop to the commercial abyss. N.W.A. would have the most profound and lasting impact on the direction of hip-hop music and its cultural milieu for the remainder of the century and into the next, and as such lays credible claim to being the most important rap group ever formed. N.W.A. began the mainstreaming of hardcore styles of gangsta rap that would reintroduce into popular culture historical representations of black males as the hypermasculine brutes and hypersexual bucks turned street-hardened gangbangers and drug dealers, told in graphic ghetto narratives involving casual black-on-black violence, drug trafficking, misogyny, and gunplay. These were bad men. Bad because they were dangerous, took what they wanted, and didn't give a fuck. Bad because they were young black men with guns shooting up the place. N.W.A.'s representation of the reformulated black brute as hardcore rapper was seen by adolescent youth as a real antisocial hell raiser, not just another rock 'n' roll bad boy wannabe. For young males—blacks, whites, indeed of many racial and ethnic stripes—hardcore rap transformed black males from the 'hood into totemic performers of a powerful masculine authenticity and identity at a time in which there appeared to be few real men left.

## Bad Men, Bad Niggers, and the World's Most Dangerous Group

N.W.A.'s street swagger only increased with the public backlash that erupted over *Straight Outta Compton*, but the *niggas with attitude* they acted out in their music and representation of black masculinity bear little resemblance to the bad man of African American folklore who was after all something of a heroic figure. Instead, N.W.A. played to the trope of the bad nigger, the social outlaw who was abhorred not only by whites, but also by blacks who knew very well that their survival depended upon getting along with whites. All concerned saw the bad nigger as a troublemaker upsetting the delicate social order.

In his book *From Trickster to Badman*, John W. Roberts makes a careful distinction between the black bad man and bad nigger in African American folkloric tradition and suggests that folk heroic traditions are typically enacted by members of subordinated groups as a counter-hegemonic act of subversion and resistance. The black bad man figure is truly heroic in the classic sense of that term because he seeks the good of those in his community and works toward that even if he is seen by whites as a troublemaker. The bad nigger, on the other hand, exerts his power by resisting all social and moral control, and tends to be viewed as a threat by other blacks since he acts in his own self-interest even if this hurts his community. Antebellum slaves who were labeled bad niggers did not simply provoke confrontation with whites by disregarding the rules of their masters and risking retribution that might also be visited upon the entire community, but were just as likely to unleash rage and violence on other blacks. Such figures were not necessarily seen as heroic by other slaves even if they stood up to white authority. After emancipation, "whites continued to view almost any black person who challenged their authority or right to define black behavior and social roles" as a bad nigger type who could be socially sanctioned or killed,[1] but these kinds of men were rarely outlaws.

Roberts characterizes Stagger Lee, the most well-known of these folkloric characters, as a bad nigger figure because he is not redeemed by his ties to the community nor does he act in their best interests. As such, the bad nigger figure is an outsider in both communities, or worse, he is an outlaw and criminal "whose very existence threatens the well-being of the society as a whole."[2] Issues surrounding social and legal control would greatly influence how African American outlaw figures would come to be viewed in society as opposed to Anglo-American outlaw figures. Roberts argues that they must be viewed differently since whites have had the luxury of viewing the law as supporting their interests and rights while African Americans have found themselves perpetually outside the law and disproportionately prosecuted. The failure of Reconstruction and the institution of Jim Crow laws in the Deep South would greatly influence conceptions of black males in the late nineteenth century. To whites, few if any distinctions were made between black males who stood up to segregation's multitude of injustices or who worked to overthrow them. What defines the bad man is that he does not abandon his own humanity in the face of inhumanity and retains the values of community, decency, fairness; he wishes for harmonious relations while he fights to usher these qualities into the world in which he lives. The bad nigger cares only for his own survival regardless of the consequences to himself or those who share his lot, and disregards the punishments for transgressing the social order they have to shoulder even if he does not. What the controversy surrounding N.W.A. revealed among blacks was how a range of considerations, including class, gender, and generational differences as well as social location, determines how these characters are interpreted at any given moment in history. For most whites, except for many adolescent males who have always found within blackness the tools of rebellion, N.W.A. merely confirmed historical fear of black males, especially those seen as exacting retribution for past grievances. In either case, N.W.A.'s representation of black maleness stood outside the boundaries of acceptable social behavior, even as performance art.

## The Sweet Science: Black Masculinity and the Performance of Aggression

The sport of prizefighting is an instructive metaphor for hardcore rap performance and the performance of masculinity and also offers some interesting parallels between these two representations of folkloric figures. Like hardcore rappers, black prizefighters engage a cultural practice that circumscribes them in terms of violence and social transgression. In this most macho of sports, some of its greatest figures over the last century have been black males who have occasionally transcended the sport and offered iconic models of powerful masculinity. For a multitude of reasons they have tended to be seen as heroic figures, or demonized, or both. The heavyweight boxer Muhammad Ali became perhaps the most reviled and revered contemporary embodiment of the folk heroic figure in the bad man mold and felt so himself inasmuch as he positioned himself as the people's champion, identifying with the struggles and ambitions of working-class blacks. Inside the ring, the fact that Ali could and did regularly brutalize white males who thought themselves his better must have been unsettling to many whites who thought the same. Outside the ring he displayed the intelligence of the street through homespun folk poetry, plain talk, and mother wit. More important, perhaps, he exercised control of his own representation of himself. Ali's outspokenness on a range of issues from the war in Vietnam to his right to worship as he pleased demonized him for many and endeared him to others. For blacks who looked up to him, he was something of a bad man because he dared to stand up to white authority and prevail within the same institutions of power that had been the tools of black oppression. To many working-class whites as well as those in institutions of state power, he certainly fit their imaginings of the bad nigger, a fact he only exacerbated when he dropped his "slave name" Cassius Clay and became a Muslim. This may have met the disapproval of many middle-class blacks as well, but he was not ostracized for it because his allegiance to community and to the fight for social justice was seen as authentic and unwavering, which allowed him to be embraced as a heroic figure by working-class and middle-class blacks alike.

Jack Johnson, on the other hand, a dominating figure in the sport from 1908 to 1915 and the first black man to win the prized heavyweight title, has quite a different legacy. He was, in the estimation of biographer Al-Tony Gilmore, truly the archetype of the twentieth-century bad nigger because he frequently challenged white expectations of black social behavior. Johnson openly flaunted his taste for flashy clothes, fast cars, and white women, but cared as little for what white authority thought of him as for what other blacks thought as well. For middle-class blacks and intellectuals he was a particular source of consternation because they were bound to defend his right as a free black man to behave as he wished even though they violently opposed him. In his biography *Bad Nigger! The National Impact of Jack Johnson*, Gilmore recalls that the African American educator Booker T. Washington publicly criticized Johnson, remarking that certain of his actions "are repudiated by the great majority of right-thinking people of the Negro race."[3]

Johnson's success, visibility, and refusal to accept the limitations of white expectation were seen as threats to the social order by both races. Convicted in 1913 under the federal Mann Act, a law created three years earlier with him in mind—he was the first person prosecuted under it, for actions committed before it was passed—Johnson was sentenced to prison but fled the country for several years, eventually returning to serve his time of a year and a day.[4] Johnson may have suffered persecution for exercising individual personal freedoms, but he was generally not seen as a heroic figure by most blacks during his lifetime. Johnson may well have regarded himself as something of a social provocateur in his own manner of doing so, but he did so by deliberately playing to type, appearing to relish taunting whites with the role they created for him, but in so doing he also ostracized himself from many in the black community who might otherwise have celebrated his professional accomplishments. Both Johnson and Ali shared the fact that their personal lives became spectacle as hypervisible black males who risked their bodies in the performance of ritualized violence. In rejecting the norms of black behavior for their times, however, they both put themselves beyond the social control of whites, and as a consequence were severely sanctioned.

Much of hardcore rap is rendered in terms of the pugilistic since it is also an arena where black males perform ritualized aggression and metaphoric violence through language. The representation of black males at the core of both endeavors centers around the spectacularized performance of the body and displays of powerful masculinity as well as a certain kind of emotional positioning that allows them to inflict suffering on another without remorse. In his article "Muscle, 'Hard Men' and 'Iron' Mike Tyson: Reflections on Desire, Anxiety and the Embodiment of Masculinity," Tony Jefferson describes this emotional positioning as "the interiorized quality extracted from risking the body in performance."[5] It is the boxer above all other sportsmen, argues Jefferson, who "remains the supreme emblem of the hard man, thus explaining boxing's macho status in the sports hierarchy."[6] Risking the body in performance is something hardcore rap performers do figuratively in a variety of performance contexts. Street-level freestyle competitions called battle rapping is the arena where up and coming rappers face off in verbal duels that mimic the spectacle of hand-to-hand combat between competing opponents, where one risks humiliation in a culture where ubermasculinity is prized. Boxing and battle rapping both involve demonstrations of masculine strength and aggression, the ability to absorb punishment and still retaliate, to overcome one's opponent by beating him down. The appeal of hardcore rap and the macho posturing characteristic of battling rapping is like boxing, masculine desire as voyeurism, part fantasy, part fetish. Jefferson confesses a fascination with Tyson's ring aggression and ability to inflict pain, something he finds himself incapable of. "In that," he writes, "I am probably like many men: drawn in by the discourse of hardness; utterly incapable of living it."[7]

The ability to identify with and embody hardness, Jefferson suggests, owes to a set of social and psychic congruencies not shared by every man. Jefferson portrays Tyson, another former heavyweight champion who was alternately revered and reviled, as the embodiment of the hard man but also as a man who allowed himself to be ultimately transformed into a beast whose public trajectory arched from a celebrated bad man to convicted rapist and bad nigger within the span of a few short years. He sees Tyson as occupying a nexus of social and emotional neglect that forged in him a quality of hardness and "a compelling satisfaction in or desire to inflict punishment" that overrides the threat of having the same punishment inflicted upon him, so that he does not fear risking his body in the performance of a brutal act.[8] Like boxing, hardcore rap portrays masculine figures risking themselves in heroic performance of verbal violence, which accounts for the aggressive nature of its lyricism and much of its macho posturing. The black male as outlaw that draws on the trope of the bad nigger may be seen alternatively as villain or folk antihero, but seldom is he viewed as a role model. N.W.A. changed that in a rather perverted sort of way.

Representations of the black male as unapologetically black, masculine, and powerful—the urban rapper-gangsta as the new *black brute cum street thug*—was a new kind of figure in American popular music. The hardcore gangsta and thug rap (re)centered the black male body into an affective economy of racial desire that, like African American blackface minstrel performers in the nineteenth century, commodified pejorative representations of themselves because satisfying demand for such images proved to be a lucrative trade. It also performed a "crucial hegemonic function, invoking the black male body as a powerful cultural sign of sexuality as well as a sign of the dangerous."[9] With the arrival of hardcore styles of rap performance, representations of black males and the display of hypermasculine black masculinity forged on the streets of the inner city began to change not simply the nature of hip-hop music, but youth perceptions of masculinity and social behavior on the street. Consequently, the rise of gangsta rap in the late 1980s and early 1990s also saw black middle-class social leaders like C. Delores Tucker aligning with white conservatives in calling for sanctions against hardcore rappers as representing the worst element within the black community.

Gangsta rap reintroduced ruptures in a black community already fractured along class lines in the wake of the civil rights era when upwardly mobile blacks who were able to get out of the inner city got out, leaving behind the poorest of poor blacks. Middle-class African Americans may have had to fight hegemonic oppression and "the image in the white mind that every black person is a potential 'bad nigger,'"[10] but disenfranchised blacks of the economic underclass often find themselves aligned against both white oppression and middle-class black sentiment. The gangsta rapper and real gang members on the street, who are often the same, feel no moral obligations to those who have left them behind. In risking themselves in performance, however, both the street hustler and those who rap about him have become romanticized figures for adolescent male rebellion. Hardcore rap music's move from an insurgent black street music into the popular mainstream is illustrative of the fact that the more rap was packaged in terms of gun-toting gangstas the bigger its suburban audiences became.

## Criminal Minded: The Allure of the Bad Nigger as Noble Outlaw

The music, culture, and iconography of hardcore gangsta rap are certainly contradictory, allowing opposing readings suggesting at times resistance to marginalization while perpetuating stereotypes rooted both in popular culture and in institutions that instantiate and legitimate notions of social deviance into imaginings around race and blackness. James Messerschmidt, in his study of adolescent gender and violence, finds that the evolution of criminology is implicated in the ways in which the human body has become linked to perceptions of violence over time and expressed in terms of both gender and racial difference. Messerschmidt examines the work of Adolphe Quetelet (1796–1874), who studied French crime statistics along with social factors like age, sex, and race, and who came "to identify the body as being somehow related to 'deviance,'" proposing that there was a "criminal man" who possessed "corporeal deviations" from what he labeled "average man."[11] Quetelet concluded that society was "threatened by the criminal body, and the body of the criminal was conceived as a sign of social dangerousness and deviation" from the normal.[12]

This deviation or deviance would later become *racialized* by Casare Lombroso (1835–1909), a founder of the science of criminal anthropology, who argues in his book *Criminal Man* that many of the bodily characteristics found in "savages and among the colored races are also to be found in habitual delinquents."[13] Lombroso defined the body, particularly the head and face, as signatures of the socially dangerous and ushered in the new science of criminology by focusing on the visible body to demarcate a corporeal difference between the criminal and the noncriminal. Messerschmidt concludes from this that bodies "are active in the production and transmission of *intersubjective* gendered meanings"[14] that are read and interpreted by other bodies. This idea has implications for thinking about performance and authenticity since notions of authenticity are often read as having to do with cultural, ethnic, or racial agency. Authenticity in terms of racial performance may be judged in terms of accountability, since "adequate participation in social life depends upon the successful presenting, monitoring, and interpreting of bodies."[15]

A spectacular example of a failed accountability in hip-hop may be seen in the case of the white rapper Vanilla Ice, who boasted about his impoverished upbringing and involvement in gang activities in order to establish street credibility as a white rap artist. When this fabrication was uncovered, Ice's reputation as a competent social agent was severely compromised. In street parlance he was "fronting," pretending to be something he was not, and so failed the test of accountability and authenticity. The white rapper Eminem, on the other hand, has more successfully played up his impoverished background and rough childhood growing up near blacks, for the same ends. He therefore has genuine accountability and credibility as a social actor that allows him to perform a kind of racialized social portraiture that signals to others his authentic intimacy with urban street culture and black masculinity. Working with former N.W.A. producer Dr. Dre gave him a kind of street credibility by association, and a number of skirmishes with the legal system including assault and weapons charges worked in his favor to paint him as a bona fide bad ass.

The Vanilla Ice episode in particular exposes how fantasies around gang violence or criminal behavior put the performance of aggression into play for those wishing to be viewed as authentic actors in the hardcore genre. Compelling tales of risk, aggression, violence, and death become privileged by rappers who may have lived the life and those that have not, so that the controlled and licensed aggression of the boxing ring is played in much the same way in the "musickal" performance, as fantasy aggression and so much braggadocio. The most prized credentials a hardcore rapper can have, street credibility and respect in addition to microphone skills, are bestowed on rappers who actually have risked their bodies in performance by engaging in violence or criminality. Sometimes it can be unclear who has crossed that line and who has not, but hardcore rap performers measure themselves by this new standard of macho and try to come off as "hard" to gain the street credibility and record sales that such representations can bestow. Rap performers since the late 1980s "have frequently been caught in a bind with respect to self-presentation, for the image of 'unabashed badness' and sexual transgression . . . sold extremely well in the twentieth century."[16] As a result, many young black males no longer challenge the demonizing stereotype of the black brute, but instead claim criminal histories as marks of distinction and authenticity that give them a legitimacy that white males, at least in the rap game, seldom possess.

If there is a redeeming note to the contemporary gangsta/thug rapper and an alternate reading of him that transcends his complicity in perpetuating the bad nigger/brute stereotype, it is in the very flaunting of black masculinity in provocative and subversive ways that resist the historical policing and containment of black male bodies, a reading that in retrospect makes Jack Johnson appear more of a socio-political provocateur than he may have been given credit for. In her book *Lockstep and Dance: Images of Black Men in Popular Culture*, Linda Tucker has suggested how black men in the United States "function within a prison writ large" structured by various methods of containment ranging from the penal system to representational practices "that criminalize their images, and render them silent and, depending on the context, either threatening or comic, hypervisible or invisible."[17] It is through various performative gestures that may be read as subversive and oppositional that black men resist this containment by acting in ways that make containment if not impossible, then certainly more difficult to maintain. The mediation of technology has made it impossible to contain urban black men to the ghettoized zones of control where they had been relegated. The language and narratives in hard and hardcore rap styles resist containment because they speak back in intemperate voices and interrogate the moral authority of those who have constructed and maintained the existence of the socio-economic ghettos that they inhabit. Technologies of visual mediation allow for the resistance and inversion of the controlling gaze so the objecti-fied black subject confronts, re-objectifies, and interrogates his observer. The twentieth-century view of the black as a tragic figure and kneeling victim, then, competes in America with an alternative view—of the hardcore rapper as a complex and problematic model of black masculinity, perhaps heroically so, arguably making him a bad man after all.

Drawing on the work of the Martinique poet and playwright Aimé Cesaire, whose 1939 book-length poem *Cahier d'un retour au pays natal* (Notebook of a Return to My Native Land) describes the narrator's return to the poverty of his childhood homeland and his identification with his degraded fellow Martinicans, Adam Lively suggests that by "embracing his blackness—not a noble blackness but the ignoble blackness, the niggerhood that is forced on him by prejudice—[Cesaire] is transfigured."[18] Cesaire's poem ultimately looks "to the future, to the 'mauvais negre,' the 'bad nigger' of the future who unlike the good nigger, the Uncle Tom, of the past will be set free by his negritude, his niggerhood."[19] Cesaire's poem from another time and place captures with persuasive clarity the oppositional ethos of the contemporary urban gangsta/thug figure, his defiance to containment and his perhaps im-passioned identification with the word *nigga*. When hardcore and thug rap-pers self-identify as "niggas," there is inherent in it a sense of inverting this rhetorical pejorative; self-defining themselves by it but subverting both its meaning and spelling (from the conventional racial epithet "nigger") converts the existential wound that induces shame and emasculation into a signifying trope of racial power, community, and resistance.

The rapper Ice Cube, for instance, probes and takes on white fear and anxiety around the black male body by proclaiming himself "the nigga you love to hate," from his provocative 1990 album *Amerikkka's Most Wanted*. Ice Cube's persona moves between the nihilistic street violence and misogynist impulses of the bad nigger and that of the bad man—a gangland outlaw turned political-minded social activist with an attitude. Because he knows it has the power to intimidate, Ice Cube wields the black male body as a weapon of retribution and transgression, turning centuries of ambivalence, fear, and derision back on his tormentors. Ice Cube assumes the subjectivity of the condemned black characters in Jean Genet's 1958 stage drama *Les Negres*, who strive for authenticity "through becoming wholly and excessively what they are—thieves, murderers, prisoners, the guilty, Negroes, 'niggers.'" For Genet, "the black man is, as [Jean-Paul] Sartre puts it, 'driven toward authenticity'" in that, insulted and enslaved, he nonetheless "draws himself up, he gathers up the word 'nigger' that has been thrown at him like a stone, he asserts himself as black, in the face of the white, with pride.' Genet's *Negres* achieve their pride by becoming, in a ritualized context, the fears and projections of the white audience. They wear the masks."[20] Genet, who aligned himself with the Black Panthers in the 1960s, had a penchant for portraying blacks as heroic criminals and prisoners in his autobiographical novels, and "was drawn to the idea of blacks embodying the alienated and dispossessed in modern society."[21] *Les Negres*, he suggests, "uses ritual, mask and parody to enact the appropriation and exorcism of prejudice. Blackness is no longer a political strategy, but an aesthetic act," and negritude was "a rite of passage leading the participants to a new state of consciousness."[22]

On the single "Amerikkka's Most Wanted," Ice Cube ritually gathers up his "niggerization" and hurls it back at his critics with his venomous first line "payback's a motherfucking nigga," which is to say that *payback is not just about getting paid, it's about niggas like me up in your face all day.* As revenge fantasy, "Amerikkka's Most Wanted" finds its power in a performative mas(k)ulinity that is not only aggrieved, but that situates Ice Cube within a community of black men who are fearless and aggressive, and who often express themselves in violent ways, the more violent, the more "authentic." For "real niggas" vulnerability is not an option. It is an emotional state reserved for their "feminine" counterparts—the gender-inclusive 'bitches" that include gay men and women, white middle-class morality, middle-class African Americans, inauthentic rappers posing as hardcore, and other "fake ass niggas." In "The Nigga You Love to Hate," Ice Cube taunts the hidden fears of whites with the line "The damn scum that you all hate/Just think if niggas decide to retaliate," which strikes at the heart of hundreds of years of policing of the black male body. In perhaps his most defiantly political statement, he addresses the prison writ large and the systematic containment of young black males who are overrepresented in the judicial and penal systems at a cost of millions of dollars while the educational uplift of a growing number of inner-city black males appears a lost battle: "You wanna sweep a nigga like me up under the rug/Kicking shit called street knowledge. Why more niggas in the pen than in college?"

## Showdown in the Terrordome:
## N.W.A. versus Public Enemy

Rap music's transition from party music into a kind of hardcore urban street-geist was not coincidental. Hardcore rap's popularity and appeal to white youth was a matter of creating a market demand and then filling that demand, a marketing strategy designed in the early 1980s by "a tightly knit group of mostly young, middle-class, black New Yorkers, in close concert with white record producers, executives, and publicists"—whose strategy rested in "its evocation of an age-old image of blackness: a foreign, sexually charged, and criminal underworld against which the norms of white society are defined, and by extension, through which they may be defied."[23] Narratives of hardness as music and as masculine representation emerge in the early 1980s with Run-DMC and later with LL Cool J. Some of Run-DMC's more political work like "It's Like That" from 1982 finds them working the terrain of the bad man, but it would be Chuck D of Public Enemy who most truly fit the heroic bad man mold. Like Run-DMC, Chuck D affected a street look and attitude that was hard-edged but that did not rely on flirting with representations of deviance or criminality. His projection of masculine power and narrative flow were used to circulate messages of socio-political empowerment and positive self-awareness that were well received by blacks and whites alike. Public Enemy would be the first group to improve on Run-DMC's urban rage and racial alienation, producing music that was more confrontational and abrasive.

The arrival of N.W.A. and Public Enemy would both signal the end of Run-DMC's reign as the dominant group in rap performance. Although they could not be more different, both groups arrived on the scene at about the same time, dropping albums in 1988 in the midst of the crack cocaine epidemic—Public Enemy hitting stride with *It Takes A Nation of Millions to Hold Us Back* and N.W.A. releasing *Straight Outta Compton*. Both groups were hard hitting, controversial, and uncompromising in their music, lyricism, and representations of black masculinity. It was music essentially made by urban black youth for other urban black youth, but both attracted sizable white followings. Both groups would also break up prematurely, but their influence on popular music would be gauged by how the industry changed after them. N.W.A. would ultimately have the most profound and lasting impact on hip-hop culture by defining West Coast hardcore gangsta rap as a new musical subgenre, while Public Enemy's socio-political music proved in the long run to be commercially unprofitable after their early and controversial demise.

Public Enemy's music was an eloquent rendering of black rage as black noise set to rhythm, 1960s revolutionary rhetoric packaged into a 1980s digital smack-down engineered by its production team the Bomb Squad. More dense and dissonant than Run-DMC's stripped-down sound, Public Enemy's production prioritized dense layering of numerous sampled loops of music combined with ambient sounds that created a cacophony of warring textures, the sonic equivalent of a race riot. Chuck D's pugilistic rhetorical jabs introduced uncompromisingly pointed commentary on race and the historical socio-political oppression of blacks in the United States. Over the range of several brilliant albums, Public Enemy rendered Run-DMC instantly anachronistic, operating in a politicized theater of militant black nationalist politics where Chuck D assertively talked back to white power. Public Enemy was the only group challenging N.W.A.'s coming dominance over the future of hip-hop culture until it self-destructed in 1989 when the group's minister of information, Professor Griff, made anti-Semitic remarks that went public. Griff was fired from the group only to be brought back. They disbanded, later to reunite, but the damage was done. The group suffered a blow to its credibility from which it would never fully recover. Public Enemy, like Run-DMC, contributed to the evolution of rapcore, a hybrid of rap and metal that can be heard in the music of the groups Rage Against the Machine, Kid Rock, Linkin Park, Limp Bizkit, Insane Clown Posse, and others, but the long-term influence of the group would not match the impact of N.W.A. in shifting the milieu of hip-hop culture and rap performance irrevocably from the hard to the hardcore. In the aftermath of the controversy, record companies apparently decided that highly politicized rap was bad for business. The political, nation-conscious rap that Public Enemy had defined was ultimately made commercially irrelevant, relegated to an alternative lifestyle on the margins of hip-hop culture as it began to mainstream on the strength of N.W.A.'s bad nigger street swagger.

## Crack Nation: The Rise of
## Hardcore Gangsta Culture and Music

The intersection of hip-hop culture, street gang culture, and drug culture created by crack cocaine in the 1980s made for a perfect storm of confluences that within a few short years—from Schoolly D's "P.S.K. What Does it Mean?" in 1985 to Dr. Dre's *The Chronic* in 1992—saw hardcore gangsta rap evolve as a subgenre of hip-hop music and quickly move into the mainstream of American popular music, where it has mutated into a number of geographical styles. Crack cocaine's intrusion into the formation of hardcore music and culture is not often discussed by music scholars, but it is nonetheless a critical discussion. The intrusion of the Cross Bronx Expressway through working-class areas of the South Bronx was a catastrophic event that precipitated the socio-cultural shifts and ruptures out of which hip-hop formed in the 1970s. Likewise, the rapid saturation of crack cocaine into inner-city ghettos must also be seen as an event with even more far-reaching consequences because it became a catastrophe of national proportions, affecting the lives of millions of mostly poor inner-city black people. It also profoundly helped to change hip-hop from a benign, party-oriented music and culture into one that was regarded as largely malevolent. In another contradiction for a musical culture that finds no shortage of them, it is inconceivable that hip-hop would have become the multibillion-dollar industry it has without the popularity of hardcore and the seminal performers that it has produced over the last several decades, including Ice-T, N.W.A., Snoop Dogg, Tupac Shakur, the Notorious B.I.G., Jay-Z, 50 Cent, and others. If there is a dark upside to the crack cocaine epidemic that raged through black communities beginning in the 1980s, arguably this is it, but it came at a tremendous cost and benefited relatively few people compared to the many more lives it destroyed.

The multimillion-dollar crack cocaine industry that swept through the inner-city streets of Los Angeles, Chicago, New York, and other large urban cities across the country in the late 1980s and early 1990s affected inner-city black populations harder than others because cocaine was largely distributed by street gangs who lived in those neighborhoods. By the early 1980s, the inner-city streets had already turned decidedly meaner than they had been in the 1970s, particularly for slum dwellers, and would soon become open drug markets and shooting galleries of internecine gang violence. Crack was primarily produced and distributed on the street by organized street units loosely affiliated with the Bloods and the Crips, two of the largest street gangs in the United States. Any number of regional groups, some highly organized such as Detroit's Young Boys Incorporated and the Chambers Brothers as well as many lesser-known gangs, distributed all around the country. On the West Coast, various factions of these gangs fought running street battles over lucrative open air drug markets located in urban neighborhoods using automatic weapons purchased with drug profits.

Conspiracy theories circulated that the U.S. Central Intelligence Agency (CIA) had deliberately and secretly dumped crack into urban neighborhoods as a plan of targeted genocide aimed at eradicating black people. There does not appear to be credible evidence that the CIA intentionally employed such a vicious policy, but there is abundant evidence that convincingly suggests crack cocaine showed up on the streets of black America as a by-product of CIA activities, specifically, the Iran-Contra scandal during the Reagan administration in the early 1980s. There is also ample information, publicly available, which suggests that officials in the U.S. intelligence community fully knew about the influx of cocaine into the United States as a result of these activities. It is now a matter of record that the U.S. government had been secretly and illegally selling arms to Iran during its long-running war with Iraq and using those proceeds to secretly and illegally fund anticommunist rebels fighting to overthrow the leftist Sandinista government in the small Central American nation of Nicaragua. The operation became the focus of extended congressional hearings in 1987 and resulted in the convictions of fourteen high-ranking officials in the Reagan administration, including Secretary of State Caspar Weinberger, National Security Agency chief John Poindexter, and his assistant, Oliver North.[24] What is now known is that many of the planes flying supplies to the Contra rebels flew back into the United States stacked with kilos of cocaine supplied by Colombian drug cartels that were distributed to black inner-city drug lords on both coasts.

In August 1996, the *San Jose Mercury News* began running a series of investigative articles on these events, identifying a Nicaraguan national by the name of Oscar Danilo Blandon, an official in the Nicaraguan government before it was overthrown by the Sandinista regime, as a central figure in the drug trafficking operation. The story, written by investigative reporter Gary Webb, was published two years later as a book entitled *Dark Alliance: The CIA, the Contras, and the Crack Cocaine Explosion*. Although Webb was discredited by the U.S. government and a number of mainstream newspapers for what they called faulty reporting, Reagan administration officials eventually admitted they knew the Contras were running drugs into the United States.[25] Other federal investigations went further. Reports by the inspector general for the U.S. Justice Department and the CIA inspector general granted that Webb's allegations had substantial merit—that there was a CIA connection between the Colombian cocaine and the crack that flooded the streets of the black inner cities in the 1980s.[26]

Much of this information is now in the public domain and available in the National Archives in Washington, D.C., as well as in a number of articles and books about the episode that largely corroborate the most damning accusations in Webb's account.[27] I have chosen to avoid the controversy surrounding Webb's book, and instead, reference similar information that appeared in the 2005 book *Freakonomics: A Rogue Economist Explores the Hidden Side of Everything*, written by University of Chicago economist Steven D. Levitt and Stephen J. Dubner, a writer for *The New York Times*. These authors, whose information has not been disputed by the government or national news media, report that Blandon acknowledges that CIA officials knew of his drug-related activities in support of raising money for the anti-Sandinista campaign. Whether that was true or not, "what *is* demonstrably true is that Oscar Danilo Blandon helped establish a link—between Colombian cocaine cartels and inner-city crack merchants—that would alter American history. By putting massive amounts of cocaine into the hands of street gangs, Blandon and others like him gave rise to a devastating crack boom. And gangs like the Black Gangster Disciple Nation were given new reason to exist."[28]

The authors of *Freakonomics* conclude that "black Americans were hurt more by crack cocaine than by any other single cause since Jim Crow"[29] since it affected such a large segment of people across a range of critical areas that help define a group's progress in a society. Within a very short time span—widespread crack use appeared in the early 1980s, spiked in 1985, and continued to escalate until 1989, when it peaked—infant mortality rose dramatically. The number of blacks sent to prison quickly tripled, and "the homicide rate among young urban blacks [thirteen to seventeen years old] *quadrupled* [emphasis in original text]. Suddenly, it was just as dangerous to live in parts of Chicago or St. Louis or Los Angeles as it was to live in Bogota.[30] The authors do not try and make a connection between crack dealers, street gang members, and hardcore rap music, but they don't need to—hardcore rappers who came up as street hustlers making their fortunes slinging rock in the 'hood (and some who perhaps did not) have provided firsthand commentary on the central role of cocaine in hardcore styles of rap over much of the last quarter century. The history of crack cocaine in hardcore rap's takeover of hip-hop culture is documented in hundreds of songs dating back almost twenty years, chronicling the birth of a street culture of drugs and drug-related gang violence that had a transforming if not defining effect on hip-hop music and culture.

The epidemic of crack circulating through black inner-city neighborhoods profoundly impacted many young black urban men and their attitudes around masculinity and interpersonal relations whether they were involved in trafficking or not, since many of them grew up in what amounted to militarized war zones. The crack trade produced "a remarkable level of gun violence, particularly among young black men, who made up the bulk of street-level crack dealers" during the peak epidemic years between 1985 and 1989.[31] The terms *gangbanger* and *drive-by* quickly became household words as a result of the unprecedented rise in urban gang violence; these themes began to appear in hip-hop songs that casually depicted street-level scenarios involving drug trafficking and gun-related homicides. The realism of such scenarios derives from the fact that since only top gang members made large sums of money in the crack trade, many street-level dealers desperate to advance "were willing to kill their rivals to do so, whether the rival belonged to the same gang or a different one. There were also gun battles over valuable drug-selling corners."[32] Typically, homicides at the height of the epidemic involved shootouts between rival crack dealers over money, territory, drugs, respect, some imagined slight, or a hundred other reasons, and where innocent bystanders were often caught in the crossfire. The result was a huge increase in violent street crime related to gangs and drugs, with one study finding that more than 25 percent of the homicides in New York City in 1988 were related to the crack cocaine trade.[33]

Whether young black males in these areas were dealing drugs, involved in gangs, or just innocent bystanders, mistrust and the adoption of hardness as a mask and a kind of street attitude became daily armor in a culture where they learned to view each other warily, since any of them were now potential assailants, targets, drug fiends, or undercover narc cops. The level of deceit, distrust, macho posturing, and violence became endemic to inner-city street culture and would eventually show up in songs that mirrored the ruptures, rifts, and ensuing "beefs" between rival gang members, hustlers, rappers, and sometimes entire organizations. The apotheosis of this phenomenon came with the highly public acrimony that developed between two of the most important hardcore rappers the music has produced, Tupac Shakur of Los Angeles' Death Row records and Notorious B.I.G. of New York's Bad Boy label. Much about the conflicts between these two men was personal and never a full blown East Coast–West Coast feud as many in the media would have it, but the dissension nonetheless ended in the assassination of both men by unknown assailants. As the line between the real and artifice became increasingly imperceptible, most of the critical records and artists that would define hardcore gangsta rap music and create a new cultural milieu around it appeared between the years 1985 and 1989, during the height of the epidemic and in the aftermath of Iran-Contra. The different ways in which hardness manifests as a critical metaphor throughout this history—as rock (street slang for crack cocaine), as attitude, as masculinity, as language, as ghetto narrative, as sound, and as imagery—suggest how critically the convergence of drugs and gangs altered the tone of the music and urban street culture. Representations of urban black males in recorded music, graphic art, magazine ads, music videos, feature films, and video games began to reformulate around notions of hardness and hard masculinity as defined by urban street culture and that began to be reflected in clothing, adornment, facial expression, body posture, and the tenor of casual interpersonal interactions. Hip-hop albums that referenced hustling, crack cocaine trafficking, gang culture, and gun violence would show up throughout the late 1980s and the 1990s and into the 2000s, and spread from the East and West coasts to other geographical regions of the country, creating a number of competing styles of hardcore rap performance.

The group that was the epicenter of this thematic narrative shift, however, was N.W.A, whose albums *Panic Zone* (1987), *N.W.A. and the Posse* (1987), and *Straight Outta Compton* (1988) contained numerous references to crack dealers and street trafficking, none more nefarious than the graphically pro-fane "Dopeman," which appeared on all three albums. Eazy-E, co-founder of N.W.A and Ruthless Records, was himself a street level crack dealer in Compton and South Central Los Angeles who used the profits to fund re-cording projects for both himself (his own solo debut album *Eazy-Duz-It* was released in 1988) and N.W.A. These groundbreaking if infamous albums put them at the very nexus of the confluence between the drug trade and the formation of hardcore rap music, contextualized within inner-city street gang culture and its ethos of masculine behavior and translated into performance art rendered in the register of the real.

## Roc Nation: Jay-Z and the Takeover of the American Dream

The apotheosis of the contemporary hardcore "crack rap" performer is un-questionably the Brooklyn-born lyrical genius Jay-Z, a former New York City drug figure turned multimillionaire entertainment mogul whose repertoire is filled with songs and lyrics that boast of his rise from "bricks to billboards" and "grams to Grammys," and who has built an empire from slinging crack in the 'hood one rock at a time. The double entendre implied in Jay-Z's Roc-A-Fella Records seems almost obscene in its celebration of capitalist excess enjoyed by the few made possible by the exploitation of the many. There is certainly irony in the fact that the label and Jay-Z's related brands—Roc-A-Wear and Roc Nation—are mainstream success stories given the scourge with which they are so blatantly associated. It is complex. It is contradictory. It is part of the story of hip-hop, which Jay-Z himself discusses candidly in his memoir *Decoded*.[34] In it, he vividly describes the allure of the hustler's life and compares that to the life of the hardcore rapper, whose narratives have so often intertwined beginning in the 1980s. As he sees it, "the story of the rapper and the story of the hustler are like rap itself, two kinds of rhythm working together, having a conversation with each other, doing more together than they could do apart."[35]

Jay-Z was not the first rapper to insert drug references into his songs; he is only one of a number of hardcore performers who, beginning with the au-tobiographical styles of Schoolly D and Ice-T in the 1980s and Tupac Shakur and the Notorious B.I.G. in the 1990s, inserted themselves into larger than life 'hood tales and drew from their own experiences as street hustlers and gang affiliates. Jay-Z also happens to have been the most successful and articulate rap artist of his generation, single-handedly reframing the ghetto fabulous street thug as the penthouse glamorous Mafioso impresario. In many ways, Jay-Z offers an instructive subject for studying the mediascape I describe in the previous chapter since he has been such a transformational figure in the evolution of contemporary hip-hop since the 1990s. His music is intensely experiential on the one hand. As he writes, his life "after childhood has two main stories: the story of the hustler and the story of the rapper, and the two overlap as much as they converge." On the other hand, he believes that the hustler's story, particularly his own, has connected with audiences on a global scale because the experience of the young black male as hustler is also part of "the ultimate human story, the story of struggle, which is what defines us all."[36] A bit hyperbolic perhaps, but it nonetheless complicates his own story and that of young black males in the United States whose lives are often determined by birth and circumstance, and this has certainly found resonance with the socio-economic struggles of others in any number of geographical locations around the world.

Jay-Z is a curious mash-up of Jack Johnson and Muhammad Ali, at once repugnant and heroic, egomaniacal and generous of spirit. The comparison between boxing and rap is not lost on him, and he in fact sees the former as a perfect metaphor for the latter. In his view, just as boxing "takes the most primal type of competition and transforms it into a sport, battling in hip-hop took the very real competitive energies on the street—the kind of thing that could end in some real life-and-death shit—and transformed them into art."[37] Jay-Z's evolutionary arc has also seen him move from a bad nigger figure to something more resembling the bad man figure, calling attention to problems as diverse as water shortages in Africa and the human suffering caused by Hurricane Katrina in New Orleans. He has, after having attained riches beyond even his own wildest fantasies, increasingly looked for ways in which to, as he puts it, be helpful.

In more than eleven studio albums beginning with 1996's *Reasonable Doubt*, the references that Jay-Z makes in his music to the gangsta/Mafioso life of hustling and drug dealing are so nuanced and artful that they appear no more ominous than a Robert De Niro gangster film, except that he is dealing in the register of the real rather than weaving the fictions of screenwriters. Jay-Z portrays himself as an entrepreneur whose beginnings as a street corner crack dealer are the stuff of Horatio Alger, no less part of the mythical American Dream than corporate robber barons or big city crime bosses. A high school dropout, Jay-Z put a new spin on the intelligent hoodlum when he showed he could step from the streets to the stage to the boardroom, for a time holding the position as CEO of Def Jam Records. His part-ownership in the New

Jersey Nets basketball team in addition to numerous other high-profile business ventures have bestowed on him the kind of mainstream credibility and prestige usually reserved for captains of Fortune 500 companies.

*Reasonable Doubt* takes a not always glamorous stroll through a hustler's life, all swagger and bravado in songs like "Can't Knock the Hustle" and "Can I Live" but exposing the human costs to one's humanity in others like "Regrets" and "D'Evils." There is a real depth of vulnerability beneath the macho posturing of the hard man evoked in many of these lyrics. Exposing that frailty, opening a window so others could see inside his soul without flinching, was a risky move for a performer who embodies the hard man persona, but it helped Jay-Z recast the hip-hop gangsta/thug as not merely a monster on the rampage (a role Tupac was sometimes all too willing to play), or a besieged man misunderstood (how the Notorious B.I.G. ultimately portrayed himself), but as an underdog who was not going to take it lying down, or, as he frames it in "Can't Knock the Hustle's" closing lines, "all these blacks got is sports and entertainment/until we even, thievin'/as long as I'm breathin'/can't knock the way a nigga eatin.'" In *Decoded* he describes the arrival of crack cocaine as "a total takeover. Sudden and complete,"[38] a generational catastrophe that saw adolescents his age serving (selling) crackheads the age of his parents, wearing automatic weapons like fashion accessories and engaging in broad-daylight shootouts over money and turf.

On his second album *In My Lifetime Vol. 1*, Jay-Z shows his hand in case anybody hearing *Reasonable Doubt* wasn't keeping up, connecting the dots between hustling street dope and spitting dope rhymes on "Rap Game/Crack Game." At times he borders on recklessness, rapping in "Real Niggaz" about clocking eightballs[39] on the corner, but it's all between the lines, coded in dense metaphor and street slang, modern-day work songs about the urban slavery of street-level hustling. Jay-Z the dope dealer and street performer embodies the brutal courage of the hard man because he risks his body in performance on the streets in a base and potentially demeaning art where his natural enemies are police, drug fiends, and rival drug dealers. Because he pushes poison on neighborhood streets knowing the powerful addictive nature of crack in particular, he arguably plays the role of the bad nigger, interested only in enriching himself and his cronies. He justifies this by arguing that he is only selling dope to dope fiends whom he does not respect anyway because they deserve none. "Crackheads," he writes, "they got no respect." Even if they were neighborhood elders, friends, and family, "once they started smoking, they were simply crackheads, the lowest on the food chain in the jungle, worse than prostitutes and almost as bad as snitches."[40]

Jay-Z the stage performer, on the other hand, transposes the physically risky act of dope peddling into the verbal aesthetic of rhyming, which carries its own risks. Because he does not write down his rhymes, Jay-Z puts himself at risk in performance because he is always essentially freestyling, the *lingua franca* of battle rapping. If flow, narrative, and drama are all part of the art of rhyming, all infused by the experiential and situational dimensions of a performer's life and daily activities, Jay-Z has crafted a vision that is coherent, almost philosophical, deeply personal, and universal in its scope. He rhymes about the narrative arc of his own life, the experiences that have made him who he is, the situations and daily drama of the hustler's life that he has used as the raw materials of aesthetic performance. His rhythmic flow is unorthodox, athletic, and dexterous, often using multiple meters or mixing them all up, jumping over bar lines as if they were prison bars trying to pen him in. It is a style carefully considered, and which he is able to penetrate and insightfully articulate for himself, writing that "sometimes the flow chops up the beat, breaks the beat into smaller units, forces in multiple syllables and repeated sounds and internal rhymes." He compares musical time and a rapper's flow to life and any individual's experience of it, an almost Zen-like metaphor that makes rhyming if not a transcendental practice (though it could be), then certainly one able to provide a space of deep introspection and the possibility of transformation. "If the beat is time," he offers, "flow is what we do with that time, how we live through it. The beat is everywhere, but every life has to find its own flow."[41] For Jay-Z, two separate flows of life— full-time hustler and part-time rapper—eventually merged into a unitary and singularly unique experience that has become the basis for his art. In his memoir, he writes that he "loved rhyming for the sake of rhyming, purely for the aesthetics of the rhyme itself—the challenge of moving around couplets and triplets, stacking double entendres, speed rapping," but that "when I hit the streets for real, it altered my ambition. I finally had a story to tell. And I felt obligated, above all, to be honest about that experience."[42]

In telling his own story, Jay-Z arguably tells the stories of many others who might be experientially like him in terms of social background and life chances, and who might also aspire to be like him, which is to say, to escape the dead end poverty of lives lived in not so quiet desperation. If hip-hop in the post–old school period had largely painted pictures of poverty, violence, and hustling, Jay-Z has sought the interiority of feeling and the actualization of human experience that Robert Plant Armstrong articulates in terms of the affecting presence, and of exteriorizing that experience. If his art resonates with authenticity, if his street credibility remains intact after a decade and a dozen platinum albums, it is because it gets inside "the interior space of a young kid's head, his psychology," and humanizes the often dehumanizing experience of being black and impoverished, of hustling street drugs for spare change and being willing to kill or die for it because the alternatives appear

no better. To create entertaining art from such narratives that retains enough
universality to find mass appeal is no small feat. Jay-Z's art is "rooted in the
truth of that experience," something he feels he owes "to all the hustlers I
met or grew up with who didn't have a voice to tell their own stories—and to
myself."[43] If Jay-Z's oeuvre appears more or less variations on a theme, he is
often trying to deepen his understanding of his own existential predicament
and that of others who identify with him, and in this way he is no less than
any other artist working within the confines of a particular aesthetic frame-
work—whether it be rondo form, the short story, or metered poetry—and
the techniques it requires. The example he offers is that of a sonnet, which
has a recurring theme and a set structure, but of which there are volumes of
variations by hundreds of romantic poets. "It's the same with braggadocio
in rap," Jay-Z observes. "When we take the most familiar subject in the history of rap—why I'm dope—and frame it within the sixteen-bar structure
of a rap verse, synced to the specific rhythm and feel of the track, more than
anything it's a test of creativity and wit," and where "there are always deeper
layers of meaning buried in the simplest verses."[44]

Braggadocio aside, Jay-Z has offered intimate and candid portraits of his
life in song, powerfully, for example, in "Renegade," where he opens up about
growing up in a broken home ("My pops left me an orphan, my momma
wasn't home") and the desperation to escape dire poverty ("I had to hustle,
my back to the wall, ashy knuckles/pockets filled with a lot of lint, not a cent")
by hustling in the street, an arena where he applied himself to a dangerous
business and earned a hardcore rap artist's most precious possession, the
street credibility of having risked his body in performance. Like the bad
nigger of black folklore, he played the outlaw, renegade as he would have it,
a kind of antiheroic figure and a powerful masculine actor who succeeded
against the odds and lived to rap about it. Jay-Z now sees himself in legendary terms, justifiably so perhaps since he changed the rap game in a number
of ways, walking the line between the urban street and the corporate world
while retaining the respect of both. He is not the first rapper from the street to
succeed in corporate America—Snoop Dogg has been pitching brand-name
products for more than two decades—but Jay-Z is the first street hustler
turned mogul to succeed at the level to which he has attained as a hit maker,
tastemaker, and pop culture icon. His last nine solo studio albums, beginning with his third in 1998, *Vol. 2 . . . Hardknock Life*, have climbed to the
top of *Billboard* magazine's 200 pop album chart as well as the R&B chart.
The release in 2009 of his eleventh album, *The Blueprint 3*, amounted to a
victory lap, reminiscing old moves over new beats and reminding everybody
how much he has helped take the hip-hop brand from the inner-city street

("oversized clothes and chains we off that/Niggaz still making it rain we off that") to Wall Street ("used to rock a throwback, ballin' on the corner/now I rock a Teller suit, lookin' like a owner") and amassing a fortune estimated at $450 million by *Forbes* magazine, which also predicts that by the end of the decade, Jay-Z will become hip-hop's first billionaire.[45]

Jay-Z's *The Blueprint 3* also gave him more No. 1 albums on *Billboard* magazine's pop charts than Elvis Presley, the man many consider to be the most important figure in the history of American popular music. The significance of that accomplishment can only be comprehended in the context of where he came from, what he overcame to get where he is, and the odds against his doing so without being killed or going to prison. Jay-Z's Horatio Alger embodies more than opportunistic entrepreneurship and the perhaps ruthless character it takes to rise to the top of the drug trade, but the idea of "hardcore smart," the rough and tumble kind of practical knowledge one acquires from the street trying to survive. In making the leap from nefarious to legitimate largely on his own terms, Jay-Z, like Muhammad Ali in the 1960s and 1970s, transformed not only his representation of himself but constructed a compelling new model of black masculinity that may have begun in brute acts but ultimately transcended them, unapologetically and with his dignity intact. Like Ali, Jay-Z escaped the "prison writ large" that polices and contains black male subjectivities by staring down white patriarchal hypocrisy and the limitations of American democracy. And, like Ali, he has lived long enough to see history stand with him.

In the song "Blue Magic" from his 2007 album *American Gangsta*, Jay-Z makes the connections between U.S. government complicity in the events that led to the explosion of crack cocaine on inner-city streets and the intrusion of narratives of drug-related violence into hip-hop culture when he rhymes "Blame Reagan for making me into a monster/Blame Oliver North and Iran-Contra/I ran contraband that they sponsored/Before this rhyming stuff we was in concert." Hyperbole aside, Jay-Z's awareness of what are now largely substantiated allegations does not mean that he excuses his own actions, but rather that he also indicts the malevolence of democratic institutions that have at various times in the history of the United States aligned themselves against the survival of the black community generally and black men in particular. The deeper causes of the crack cocaine epidemic, he writes in *Decoded*, "were in policies concocted by a government that was hostile to us, almost genocidally hostile when you think about how they aided or tolerated the unleashing of guns and drugs on poor communities, while at the same time cutting back on schools, housing, and assistance programs. And to top it all off, they threw in the so-called war on drugs, which was really a war on us."[46]

Nonetheless, Jay-Z's brutality and risk taking as a hard man has always fit more the pattern of the bad nigger than the bad man, championing only his own ambition and the struggle to escape grinding underclass poverty by grinding out rocks until he could move up to pushing real weight, kicking it all back into the chance of making a shot for himself to go straight as a rapper. Like the black outcasts in Jean Genet's *Les Negres* who sought authenticity through becoming wholly and excessively what they were—thieves, murderers, prisoners, the guilty, Negroes, niggers—Jay-Z and many like him drew themselves up in defiant if risky and destructive behavior with the realization that "the world don't like us/is that not clear." Consequently, after the crack explosion, the hustler's life became the meta-narrative of hip-hop when young black men made the connection between hustling dope and hustling dope beats—you could use the one to finance the other and hopefully graduate from one game to the next. As Jay-Z recalls, "a lot of people came to hip-hop like that, not out of a pure love of music, but as a legit hustle, another path out of the 'hood."[47] Jay-Z would appear to have few regrets in this regard judging by the line from his song "What We Talking About," also from *The Blueprint 3*: "As far as street guys we was dealin' crack/That's just how the game goes I don't owe nobody jack."

The reality has always been more complicated, and perhaps part of Jay-Z's genius and appeal is that he has managed to complicate the lives and struggles of young black males whom others are quick to read as no better than two-dimensional. Part of Jay-Z's personal narrative has always been about carrying the weight of regret, the ability to live with the consequences of bad choices and to keep moving forward. It is a theme he has articulated in some way since *Reasonable Doubt*, an album he ended with a song entitled "Regrets" ("This is the number one rule for your set/In order to survive, you gotta learn to live with regrets") and to which he gives perhaps its most eloquent rendering in *Decoded*, where one of the annotations to that song suggests a full awareness of the contradictions that haunt his humanity: "I wanted to end [*Reasonable Doubt*] with regret, that last feeling you have before you go to sleep, or feel when you wake up and look at yourself in the bathroom mirror."[48]

As a successful entrepreneur, Jay-Z can now—as other robber barons before him—afford the luxury of philanthropy. In this regard, he has begun to assume more the position of the bad man who looks after a community of others outside his circle. Besides raising money for victims of Hurricane Katrina, he joined UNICEF and MTV in 2006 to make the video documentary *Diary of Jay-Z: Water for Life* to raise awareness about the problem of severe water shortages in Africa, and put on free concerts to get young people involved in the 2008 presidential campaign behind the candidacy of Barack Obama.

Besides employing hundreds of people through his various enterprises that include the multimedia entertainment conglomerate Roc Nation, his efforts to help build a new stadium for the New Jersey Nets basketball team and bring them to Brooklyn may also be seen as beneficial to the community (his part-ownership has been touted in promotional ads raising the team's public profile) though it profits him handsomely as a business venture. Perhaps few begrudge Jay-Z his success given his undeniable talent and business acumen, but his path to fame and riches remains problematic since it does not take into account the number of dead crackheads he has left in his wake or the number of young black males who will try to follow his path and fail.

Jay-Z and other African American hardcore rap performers who work a brute trade have transformed the dynamics, contradictions, and often tragic ironies of their own lives and life experiences into ritual play and entertainment that many adolescent males find as alluring as other forms of violence-oriented entertainment in popular culture. Nonetheless, the downside certainly is that hardcore rap music and its street-oriented cultural milieu construct a grotesque theater of the absurd where the boundary between the real and performance is ever shifting and quite arbitrary, and where there is often little difference between the stage, the studio, and the street. Because hardcore rap performers *do* construct their personas and narratives in the register of the real, this has tended to bestow upon them the credibility that goes with authenticity, even if that authenticity explores black rage as the nihilistic brutality of street violence, drugs, and gangbanging. Ghetto narratives and 'hood tales involving a legion of bad nigger figures have come to be seen as having universal appeal without the entanglement of politics and polemics associated with socially conscious bad men types who descend from the Native Tongues lineage. The racial politics of Public Enemy ultimately proved bad for business, so that "by the turn of the century, to be labeled a 'conscious' or 'political' rapper by the music industry was to be condemned to preach to a very small choir"[49] and to a relatively small share of hip-hop's hugely profitable mainstream commercial market. This is not to say that many hardcore rappers, young black males from the street with few life chances who *have* risked their bodies in performance, are not aware of the existential dilemma in which they find themselves—to hustle bricks or hustle rhymes—even though success at the latter is often contingent upon success at the former. The fact that they *can* self-reflexively transform their real-life narratives into artifice and art suggests that they are conscious social actors who know their stories are more real than most, and that this is what gives them appeal and credibility.

Importantly, what hardcore styles of rap in particular have helped to do is reinforce the powerful ways in which language, emotion, music, blackness, and the body intersect at dangerous crossroads that are circulated in a contemporary context of global exchange that "retains residual contradictions of centuries of colonialism, class domination, and racism."[50] Ideas of blackness and masculinity derived from hip-hop music and culture all circulate as commodities in a global marketplace that does not necessarily reflect relations of reciprocity and mutuality when participants in that dialogue "speak from positions of highly unequal access to power, opportunity, and life chances."[51] The ways in which hardcore styles of rap are perceived and consumed have arguably had a deleterious effect on how black people and black culture are viewed not only in the United States but in other parts of the world even though this in itself is not new. Modernist literature, art, and music in the West have "consistently spectacularized difference, titillating 'respectable' audiences with sensational portrayals of 'primitive,' 'exotic' and 'oriental' outsiders"[52] who are nonetheless perceived as frightening exactly because they are objectified and rendered in terms of the grotesque. The problem is certainly complicated when those being portrayed are also participants in the construction of their own spectacularization and objectification. In this case it is fair to ask whether the selling of stereotypes of difference by those who *are* different constitutes the selling out of innocents who see no compensatory benefits from such Faustian deals with the devil.

A larger issue, perhaps, is whether Jay-Z and other artists who have made their names in a vile trade must ultimately bear the burden of what I call a "Bert Williams problem." What I mean is that, even though these artists are lavishly paid and many of them admired by fans and respected by peers, and while they have opened up enormous doors of commerce and opportunity for those with the talent and grit to follow them, the question of whether their cultural productions and philanthropy do enough to counterbalance the empty space in the representation of black masculinities left in their wake remains a serious one. The most egregious consequences of perpetuating historically pejorative meta-narratives of black males—of reinserting the bad nigger into contemporary popular culture, of making hustling appear to be a viable life choice even in the face of nothing better—are likely to last beyond their own careers and well into the future. Few people outside black music historians and serious fans of hardcore rap may have ever heard the name Schoolly D, yet his influence on the direction of hip-hop music and popular culture continues to be lasting and profound a quarter century on. In the final chapter I discuss the predictable consequences of such cultural productions in terms of what other social actors choose to emulate, as well as some perhaps alternative routes.

## 5. Race Rebels

### Whiteness and the New Masculine Desire

In "The Problem with White Hipness," Ingrid Monson has suggested how certain affectations that signified and indexed the cool and the hip became associated with black avant-garde jazz musicians from late 1940s bebop culture, and which appeared to reject white mainstream conformity through a music and lifestyle viewed as socially deviant and therefore liberatory. The jazz culture of bebop would inspire the bohemianism of the white hipster and the beat poets and writers of the 1950s that included Jack Kerouac, William Burroughs, Allen Ginsberg, and other socially alienated white intellectuals. Through the adoption of modes of black male expressive behavior—slang-laden speech, rhythmic black music, flamboyant dress, a new vocabulary of body gestures, and an attitude of aloofness that rejected the conformity of the "square" world—the white hipster reproduced the *affecting black presence* through manner and style as racialized performance in which "the attitude of the bebop musician as anti-assimilationist social critic became embodied in and visualized through various sonic, visual, linguistic, and ideological markers."[1] These markers became affective qualities associated with the black body in performance and were eventually appropriated and (re)presented in formulations of social identity and expressions of powerful masculinity for white males in popular culture not only in music but in other mediums, particularly film.

Monson argues that through such superficial engagements "the idea of hipness and African American music as cultural critique" has become detached from the "socially conscious attitude that hipness has been presumed to signify."[2] Liberal white hipsters fall into a trap, she suggests, by viewing blackness as a kind of absence, for instance, of a morality that African Americans are presumed to lack and that defines them as perpetual social outsiders, and which "paradoxically, buys into the historical legacy of primitivism and its concomitant exoticism of the 'Other.'"[3] Monson apparently believes that white assumptions about black primitivism, deviance, and morality are somehow coincidental, which would overlook the fact that the racial imaginings of whites have always drawn upon tropes of primitivism and exoticism of the black Other. Perhaps what she means to suggest is that it is rather paradoxical that these cool, urbane, and sophisticated black actors whose sense of how enlightened human beings ought to interact with each other should somehow be read as primitive because the music they performed was as visceral as it was intellectual. In any case, Monson does not fully take into account the very real allure of notions of deviance and primitivism in the formation of white adolescent male identity, a matter certainly not lost on Norman Mailer in his construction of the white hipster.

The socially conscious attitude that Monson suggests black hipness presumes to signify has arguably been less a critical factor in the adoption of aesthetic markers of black style by middle-class white youth than has been the association of such gestures with quaint notions of class revolt, the liberation from pseudo-Victorian mores, and the fetishization of the black Other as a radical social actor. In the same way that minstrel performance created liberatory spaces in which white actors could critically engage their apprehension and fears surrounding the complexities and contingencies of pre-industrialization and a rapidly shifting social order, subsequent appropriations of black subjectivity have served much the same role. When Monson eventually engages the ways in which stereotypes of blackness have historically been associated with madness, pathological sexuality, and deviance, she appears to suggest understanding all along, particularly when she acknowledges that white hipsterism and the performance of black masculinity have everything to do with the "bald equation of the primitive with sex, and sex with the music and body of the black male jazz musician."[4] Dizzy Gillespie's cool style and mannerisms—his horn-rimmed glasses, goatee, and French beret—were widely imitated by white hipsters because they were read as subversive.[5] Monson also acknowledges that "the 'subcultural' image of bebop was nourished by a conflation of the music with a style of black masculinity that held, and continues to hold, great appeal for white audiences and musicians."[6] However, it is not simply the case that black bebop musicians found themselves subjected to appropriation by primitivist racial ideologies, but that the black body itself has been prone to such cultural appropriations ever since T. D. Rice jumped Jim Crow. In the end, Monson concludes that the association of African American males with criminality and general mayhem "sold extremely well in the twentieth-century."[7] The triumph of hardcore rap makes it clear that the transgressive black body, primitivism, and cross-racial desire continue to find value in the marketplace of global popular culture well into the new millennium.

## Elvis Rocks the White Negro

The conflation of styles of music with representations of black masculinity and sexuality has been a recurring trope in American popular culture and in the construction of white working-class identity. It is arguable whether 1950s rock 'n' roll could have become the cultural phenomenon it did without the interpretive power and appeal of Elvis Presley, who made palpable connections between the corporeal body, black male subjectivity, sexual transgression, and social rebellion. Elvis was the quintessential white hipster and the rock 'n' roll body personified, defining and telegraphing through movement, gesture, deportment, and stylish couture the art of social subversion for white middle- and working-class youth.

There was nothing particularly subversive about the music Elvis sang during his period in Memphis with Sam Phillips' Sun Records but the fact that he sang it at all, and that he sang it "with the Negro sound and the Negro feel" borrowed from his love of black gospel and rhythm and blues that Phillips had been searching for in a white singer. Bill Haley and the Comets had already created the synergy of country music and rhythm and blues that became rock 'n' roll in cover versions of songs such as "Rock Around the Clock" and "Shake Rattle and Roll" before Elvis ever cut his first side, a cover of Arthur "Big Boy" Crudup's "That's All Right, Mama" (omitting the word "Mama") in July 1954. What became important in Elvis' appeal, besides the fact that he was a decent singer, were his matinee idol good looks, a youthful raciness, and the fact that he essentially represented and made available to white audiences a performance of sexualized black male subjectivity that removed the taboo of race. With his famous sneer, flamboyant dress, and sexually suggestive performance of the body, Elvis became the new and improved racialized Other, leading a full-frontal assault on the last vestiges of Victorian decorum once assailed by the minstrel mask.

Elvis' emotive sexual power was informed by his interpretation of a now implicit black male subjectivity that erased the visible sign of blackness that in minstrelsy was represented by the act of masking. If there is any sense to John Lennon's curiously naïve remark that "before Elvis, there was nothing," it is perhaps that before Elvis, white teen males had no masculine models that could transpose with any real authenticity the swagger of black males onto white bodies. Elvis' authenticity rested not in the mojo of the blackface mask but in his transfiguration of the sexualized and spectacularized black male body, gyrating his famous pelvis in such a publicly vulgar way that it might well be considered the 1950s version of crotch grabbing. In any case, Elvis pointed his compass in the right direction, below the belt where the good stuff is, thus forever linking the new music of social rebellion with sex, the masculine body, deviance, and a subtext of underlying associations around primitivism and blackness. Presley was as predictable and perhaps as necessary as Al Jolson, Paul Whiteman, or Benny Goodman before him, since each represented a solicitous devotion to black cultural appropriation and consumption that, perhaps paradoxically, coexisted with a disingenuous impulse to erase the black body from virtually every other aspect of American life.

Presley's charisma, looks, and good-natured innocence, along with a genuine affinity for black music and culture, allowed him to believably assume black male subjectivity as racialized performance, and like T. D. Rice, interject it metaphorically into the field of popular culture as community property. Presley's enduring contribution to the popularization of rock 'n' roll may also have had more to do with the fact that he gave white adolescents (perhaps for the first time since Frank Sinatra in the 1930s but certainly with more abandon) permission to engage themselves emotionally to the point of hysteria, and in a very public way. For girls this largely manifested as euphoric screaming, sobbing, and amorous swooning. For adolescent males this meant the adoration of emulation. Presley provided the template for a new model of masculine performance that was emotive and vulnerable yet boldly and bodily assertive.

In either case, such affective displays were predicated on a certain amount of licensed abandon that Presley made available through the appropriation of performative modes of dress, gesture, speech, vocal delivery, and body-ism that were exuberantly liberating. Rock 'n' roll of the 1950s was "a place where excess [was] glorified [and where] the body [was] released from surveillance and societal control; screaming and yelling, as at an Elvis concert, [was] not only sanctioned, but encouraged."[8] With Elvis, the appropriation of rhythm and blues and black male subjectivity become transfigured in a sleight-of-hand racial performance that transformed white youth into rock 'n' roll rebels and alienated social outsiders, portrayed in Hollywood films by actors such as Marlon Brando and James Dean. Presley's mastery of "transvesting,"[9] in which one wears the clothing and assumes the identity of another, inverted the play of black and white subject positions that were the ground of minstrelsy performance. In blackface performance, the Janus-faced image of the black mask externalizes blackness as a kind of *explicit actor* while whiteness remains internalized, literally invisible, as an informing albeit implicit *internal actor*. It is the mask that imbues the performance with authenticity while whiteness remains presumably untainted behind the illusion it has created for itself. In this play of the carnivalesque, the black body is the thing made visible. Tattered clothing, a caricature of black speech patterns, facial gestures, the motioning of the hands, jig dancing, and other performative gestures work in tandem to construct a representation of black male subjectivity as theatrical spectacle encoded at the site of the body while the minstrel performer as provocateur and puppet-master winks from behind his fool's mask. The performance of the black body in minstrelsy references, then, an array of cultural practices that both erase and (re)present black subjectivity as an externalized phantasm of the white racial imagination.

The black minstrel introduced into white American working-class culture ideas and emotions that could not have been otherwise articulated safely, thus mapping out for the white performer new ways of emotionally relating to an otherwise rigid and restricted world. In *Sambo: The Rise & Demise of an American Jester*, Joseph Boskin underscores the importance of affective appropriation in racial transvesting by suggesting that "the Caucasian feel for black styles was enormously enhanced and widened by the minstrel's complex utilization of the black experience"[10] in an array of allusive ways that constructed an illusion of authenticity. The focus on feel, on emotion and affective performance, is of paramount importance, as are the ways in which it is captured, transposed, and inscribed from black to white bodies, where it is then rearticulated in such a way that whiteness itself becomes transfigured. With Presley, bodily gestures, movements, and a provocative performance style that mimicked the exuberance and emotional energy of black performers become visual signifiers that replaced masking as the affective apparatus constructing the illusion of black subjectivity. White subjectivity now becomes externalized, literally liberated from the duplicitous deceit of the blackface mask as well as from social constraints that repressed physical displays of emotional exuberance. The freedom to openly exult in emotive ways would have been as liberating for British youth throwing off the last vestiges of postwar Victorianism as for white American youth growing up in Dwight Eisenhower's America, which certainly explains Lennon's sycophantic gratitude—the hysteria of "Beatlemania" in the 1960s could not have happened without Elvis a decade earlier.

White rock 'n' roll performers also negotiated intractable tensions around race mixing that lay at the heart of much of the early opposition to rock 'n' roll, which "represented everything that white, middle-class parents feared:

it was urban, it was sexual, and most of it was black."[11] The sexual fantasy and adoration of infatuated teenage girls that rock 'n' roll unleashed were perhaps more tolerable if the objects of their adoration were Elvis, Jerry Lee Lewis, and Pat Boone because it stemmed fears of miscegenation. Russ Sanjek, a vice president of the music-licensing agency Broadcast Music, Inc (BMI), recalled the golden age of rock 'n' roll as "a time when many a mother ripped pictures of Fats Domino off her daughter's bedroom wall. She remembered what she felt toward her Bing Crosby pin-up, and she didn't want her daughter creaming for Fats."[12]

## Ways of Knowing: The Politics of Racial Border Crossings

The black body has typically been appropriated and deployed as a kind of discursive text that constitutes a web of cultural connotations inscribed with an array of possible meanings that are then (re)inscribed onto white bodies and performed in ways that signify powerful historical ideologies about blackness, gender, masculinity, and personal power—ideological articulations that are "used by . . . fans to construct identities that provide alternative representations of their real social experiences."[13] These ways of apprehending blackness and masculinity have become critical to ongoing efforts by white youth to "represent their own experiences, to speak in their own voices rather than in the hegemonic codes"[14] of mainstream culture and its repressive social constraints.

George Lipsitz also observes that while the disguise of blackness in minstrelsy performance ministered to deeper needs and desires of both performers and audiences, it "is still important to understand how and why the fascination with difference works."[15] In Lipsitz's assessment, "the genius of African-American culture in nurturing and sustaining moral and cultural alternatives to dominant values has made it an important source of education and inspiration to alienated and aggrieved individuals cut off from other sources of oppositional practice."[16] This notwithstanding, he argues, the suffocating kinds of social tyranny that youth seek to escape through such appropriations should also encourage more principled and perhaps more productive engagements across cultures than those based on caricature and stereotype. In the historical evolution of American assimilation, whiteness had more to do with class privilege than with notions of nationality or physiology, and was something purchased and fought for by Jews, Catholics, Irish, Italians, Polish, and indentured servants, while blackness "was never something one had to attain, at least not outside of Bohemian circles."[17] Given this history, constructions of whiteness that rely on the fetishization of the racial Other must continually be interrogated since they retain the power to perpetuate commodity racism and racial exploitation.

Lipsitz offers a number of examples of progressive engagements in racial culture crossings, among them the Greek American rhythm and blues musician Johnny Otis, who participated so fully in the life of the black community that he became "black by persuasion."[18] Lipsitz also offers the examples of white jazz musician Bix Beiderbecke, whose lyrical brilliance on the cornet was the only real rival to Louis Armstrong; the Jewish American salsa musician Larry Harlow, acclaimed by Latino audiences as El Judio Maravilloso (The Marvelous Jew); and the Euro-American singer Johnnie Ray, who grew up in a white Protestant farm family in Oregon and who became attracted to black music because of a disability. For these musicians, Lipsitz argues, black music provided them with the means of making a powerful critique of mainstream, middle-class Anglo-Saxon American culture as well as with an elaborate expressive vocabulary for rendering their own feelings of marginality and contestation. Lipsitz poses a number of intriguing questions around contentious issues such as appropriation, authenticity, empathy, and ethics around the consequences of cultural collusion and collision: Which kinds of cross-cultural identification advance emancipatory ends and which reinforce existing structures of power and domination? When does identification with the culture of others serve escapist and irresponsible ends and when does it encourage an enhanced understanding of one's experiences and responsibilities? Popular culture's propensity for serving as a site for experimentation with new identities offers opportunities as well as dangers, since thinking of identities "as interchangeable or infinitely open does violence to the historical and social constraints imposed on us by structures of exploitation and privilege."[19]

On the other hand, Lipsitz is wary of essentialist arguments that assume innate and immobile identities for ourselves or others and that confuse history with nature, thus denying the possibility of real change. Those observations notwithstanding, he finds fault with intercultural collaborations by superstar pop musicians such as Paul Simon's 1986 *Graceland* and David Byrne's 1989 *Rei Momo* because they obscure unexamined relations to power and delight in difference as a process organized around exotic images from overseas. Such collaborations, he suggests, offer no corollary inspection of their own identities, but rather comprise escapes into postmodern multiculturalism that hide the privileges, evasions, and contradictions of whiteness in America. He contrasts that to the 1970s rock band Redbone, composed of a Native American from an Indian reservation in Washington state and two Mexican American brothers who grew up in Fresno, California, and who became "Indian" based largely on their cultural and political identification with Native

American issues. The band immersed itself in Native American imagery and identity through stage costumes, borrowings from Native American music, and highly political lyrics that referenced the sacred Ghost Dance, the U.S. Army massacre of Lakota Indians at South Dakota's Wounded Knee, and the American Indian Movement's (AIM) ongoing battles with the Bureau of Indian Affairs, becoming in Lipsitz's estimation, the first fully self-conscious, self-affirming, and visible Native American rock band. Redbone's example of empathy as "a way of knowing, and of transcending space and time to connect with other people," is non-exploitative and socially progressive, since it "also entails understanding and acknowledging the things that keep us divided. It demands that we take responsibility for our social locations and make our choices accordingly."[20]

The same alienation that perhaps drove a despairing Bix Beiderbecke in the 1920s or a rejected Johnnie Ray in the 1950s to seek succor in black music no doubt compels some contemporary young whites to embrace the moral and political messages of hip-hop. Just as often, however, these kinds of ethical cultural appropriations tend not to be the case. Rather, the performance of black modes of expressive behavior by many white male social actors in hip-hop in particular have tended to be driven by commodity fetishism and the kind of racialized desire that reduces black subjectivity to stereotype. These appropriations have certainly been aided and abetted by the construction and performance of masculinities that have tended to be socially alienating as in the case of hardcore hip-hop and where an array of artfully produced noise, particularly in the late 1980s, created "the backdrop for powerful depictions of gang life on the streets of Los Angeles"[21] and other American cities at a time that also saw a rise in street violence related to the crack cocaine wars.

The swagger of the hardcore gangsta rapper and the street-level crack dealer as late twentieth-century antiheroic cultural icons (re)located urban black male subjectivities as sites of horrific violence and tremendous power that would challenge models of masculinity from rock 'n' roll. When MTV debuted in 1981 with blow-dried white rockers in leather spandex stroking electric guitars, these images offered perhaps the most powerful and spectacularized representations of masculinity and the male body to white male adolescents since 1950s rock 'n' roll. These ideas, images, and meanings constructed an affective apparatus around mainstream rock that made it empowering and gave it meaning to white adolescent youth. This apparatus of visuals, sounds, instruments, and phallic-laden symbolism constructed rock music as particularly masculine, and, with few exceptions since the early 1960s, rock has been the arena in which fantasies of white masculine identity have been played out. Heavy metal music and culture forge a performance of masculinity through the use of certain instruments (the guitar most prominently), dress, lyrical content, and performance styles. These combine to form a certain quality of affective energy expressed as masculine power, and which may be seen as reflexively empowering to the performer.

The hardness, aggression, and hypersexuality associated with heavy metal are intrinsically related to the formation of gender identity and masculine empowerment for young white males who listen to this music and who participate in the culture. The bad boy affectations of white rock performers had taken social rebellion and subversion as far as they could by the time hard styles of rap showed up. When rap bumrushed MTV's suburban demographic after the ascent of Run-DMC, the black male body and the hard-edged street realism of its cultural milieu began to replace the white male body and the cartoonish parody of machismo depicted in 1980s glam and "cock rock" as the site of spectacularized displays of masculinity. Hardcore rap performance was not simply a facsimile of bad boy attitudes and behavior, it offered something more. This was not Mick Jagger's jerky chicken walk and goofy sneer meant to reference Elvis and suggest nonconformist ways of moving and behaving. Hardcore rap was the real thing—ghetto realism that dramatized West Coast gang culture, the scourge of crack cocaine, drive-by shootings, black rage, and nihilism in the nation's disintegrating inner cities all played out against ghetto fabulous images of money, cars, and women. Rap had already begun to be constructed as a more masculinist form of performance since the emergence of Run-DMC in the mid-1980s, and by the early 1990s hardcore rap videos had (re)created the black male body as a new and powerfully alluring site of masculine desire as hardcore rap performance moved into the popular mainstream.

## New Kids in the Ghetto: The Beastie Boys Get Ill

The concurrent rise of hip-hop and video culture meant that the new language of male body-ism based in the vernacular of black urban street style would become quickly and broadly available to a diverse demographic of young males. That notwithstanding, the number of white males able to find success as hip-hop performers dramatically diminished in the years following Dr. Dre's 1992 *The Chronic*, which set the stage for hardcore black rappers with undeniable street credibility such as Snoop Dogg, Ice Cube, the Notorious B.I.G., Tupac Shakur, and others, to up the ante for authenticity, masculine performance, and real-life street narratives. The mainstreaming of ubermasculine macho posturing, and the rejection of the feminine substantially drove women from the microphone and made it more difficult for white males to compete as well. Up until then, despite the difficulties inherent in negotiating a music dominated by urban African Americans and Latinos,[22] hip-hop had produced a first generation of white acts such as Vanilla Ice, 3rd Bass, House of Pain, Markie Mark (the actor Mark Wahlberg), Young Black Teenagers, and the Beastie Boys, all of whom helped attract a large white youth follow- ing to hip-hop. None of these were hardcore acts per se, as none of them had the street experiences that would lead them to convincingly sustain such illusions. Nonetheless, all of them more or less deployed affective strategies such as street beats, aggressive masculine posturing, baggy urban street at- tire, and an *in your face* attitude (telegraphed by pernicious mean mugging) of aesthetic combat through rhyming and dissing other MCs that at least put them in the game. Of these acts, however, only the Beastie Boys would survive into the gangsta and thug rap era and the new culture of masculinity that emerged at the end of the 1980s.

A New York City–based trio of Jewish kids who had musical roots in punk, the Beastie Boys would become the first white group to make it as a rap act on the strength of their 1986 album *Licensed to Ill*. The record got them noticed by major critics, largely positively if controversially, and became the first rap album to top the *Billboard* 200 pop chart in the United States, also rising to the No. 2 spot on the R&B album chart. The fact that the Beastie Boys lasted for more than two decades while continuing to produce good records (their 2004 album *To the 5 Boroughs* was their first to simultaneously top both the *Billboard* 200 and R&B/Hip-hop album charts as well as the European and Internet album charts) and selling out concert halls without substantially changing who they are speaks to an aura of credibility and a solid fan base that few hip-hop performers black or white have been able to sustain. The Beastie Boys' self-deprecating humor and adolescent pranksterism at times appear to parody if not caricature both rap and punk, and their early live shows often took on an air of comic surrealism and the absurd—semi-nude women dancing in cages, giant inflated penises, obscenity-laced shouting matches with hecklers—that pushed the boundaries of good taste and oc- casionally legality, resulting in brawls, arrests, and lurid headlines, all of which played to the group's frat boy party ethic and bad boy image, making them perhaps the Sex Pistols of the hip-hop generation. It also gave them incredible "street cred"—three Jewish kids on the bad nigger tip.

*Licensed to Ill* could not be considered hardcore in the sense that the term would come to mean, and the notion that the Beasties set the precedent for gangsta rap, as some might argue, is merely quaint. Schoolly D had already released the seminal singles "Gangster Boogie" in 1984 and "P.S.K. What Does It Mean?" in 1985, and Ice-T's 1986 single "6 in the Morning" had offered a more brutal and realistic portrait of urban violence and street gang life than anything the Beasties could have imagined. Nonetheless, the Beastie Boys were the first rap group to capture mainstream media attention and top the pop charts with songs involving casual violence, gunplay, references to drug use, and misogynistic material that formed the core of hardcore styles, and in that sense they certainly cracked open the door that black hardcore rappers, many of them real gangsters, would eventually bumrush.

The body-ism of the Beasties did not project the same intensity of aggressive, streetwise masculine posture affected by black male performers such as LL Cool J, Run-DMC, Ice-T, Schoolly D, Ice Cube, Eazy-E, Snoop Dogg, and others, but it certainly drew more from the expressive body gestures of inner-city black and Latino males than it did from punk rock or heavy metal. The Beasties' lyrics were relatively free (though not completely so) of the kind of graphically violent, sexual, and scatological language that hardcore rap would virtually normalize, but they nonetheless trafficked in controversial themes and language that were more objectionable than anything Run-DMC and LL Cool J were attempting at the time. On the other hand, the Beasties shared the new school style of hard, sampled drum machine beats and aggressiveness in attacking the microphone that Run-DMC and LL Cool J had adopted, owing certainly to connections they shared with these performers through Def Jam Records, Russell Simmons, and Rick Rubin.

The Beasties retained enough of their punk rock origins that gratuitous sex and drugs, raunchy lyricism, and bad behavior would be par for the course in anything they were likely to do, but by adopting the aesthetic practices associated with hip-hop they helped to legitimate the public performance of social deviancy in mainstream hip-hop two years before N.W.A.'s arrival. Their ethnic Jewish heritages notwithstanding, they also did not have to navigate the problem of the racial Other at the same time that they were rapping about sex, drugs, and violence inasmuch as most ethnic European immigrant identities in the United States had gradually been subsumed under the rubric of whiteness in the years before and following World War II. Nonetheless, racial subtext and the *absent black presence* were always animating features of how the Beastie Boys formed their public personas, and which helped give them a ground of authenticity that proved durable and appealing to a diverse audience. In many of their most celebrated songs, including those on *Licensed to Ill*, the Beasties gave tongue-in-cheek shouts out to urban 'hood tales and gangsta-themed narratives that resonated with black and white fans alike. Their ability to cross the racial divide by performing in a black urban music style and doing it credibly earned them a devoted following among suburban white male adolescents and the admiration of black hip-hop performers for whom they opened up the market for hardcore just as Elvis opened up the market for black rhythm and blues.

The Beastie Boys' upper-middle-class backgrounds and privilege, however, hardly lent themselves to the kinds of antics they portrayed on record. Their song "The New Style" starts out as innocent braggadocio, a throw-down aimed at rival MCs that gets about as graphic as the Beasties were likely to get ("Got rhymes that are rough and rhymes that are slick/I'm not surprised you're on my dick"), but as language goes in hardcore rap, hardly warrants bleeping by comparison, though in the recording they slightly obscure the phallic reference in order to lessen its full audible impact (did they say *dick* or an elongated "d"?), but it was clear enough what was meant, so that the per-ceived use of an obscenity was seen as daring, as indeed it was for a rap album that entered the pop mainstream. A few lines later, however, the rhymes take a darker turn ("Father to many, married to none/And in case you're unaware I carry a gun/Stepped into the party, the place was over packed/Saw the kid that dissed my homeboy and shot him in the back") but did not generate a great deal of public outrage beyond the Parents Music Resource Center. The Beastie Boys' crudeness, luridness, and misogynistic impulses may have been viewed as sophomoric and objectionable at the time, raising middle-class hackles, but they did not invite the kind of public condemnation and panic that would follow the arrival of N.W.A. just two years later.

Likewise, instances of drug use are rife in Beastie Boys songs but are put forth with more levity than gravity, such that they did not draw especially widespread public criticism. The popular song "Hold It Now—Hit It" is a party anthem that revels in drinking prodigious amounts of everything from Heineken to Thunderbird, but also boasts of "friends in high places that are keeping me high." A few lines later they are "Hip-hop, body rockin' doing the do/beer drinking, breath stinking, sniffing glue," while near the end the narrator raps "I take no slack 'cause I got the knack/And I'm never dusting out 'cause I torch that crack," some of the earliest pop culture references to the street drugs angel dust and crack cocaine at a time most Americans had never even heard of these drugs. As far as the treatment of women went, the Beastie Boys were not merely reprehensible but a harbinger of what was to come. Lines such as "I'm the king of the classroom, cooling in the back/My teacher had beef so I gave her a smack" from "Slow Ride" suggest the wave of misogynistic violence that would soon become fashionable in the popular mainstream with the rise of hardcore gangsta rap.

If the success of the Beastie Boys may be seen as problematic, it is because they used black music to act out for white audiences the brutish stereotypes of lewdness and violence historically associated with black males that had been a subtext in the formation of rock 'n' roll. On the other hand, if their performance of white Negroism had an air of authenticity to it, it was because their behavior represented more or less who they were in real life—in Russell Simmons' characterization, "three white kids who didn't give a fuck." The Beastie Boys obviously loved hip-hop music, just as had many Jewish entertainers before them (Eddie Cantor, Symphony Sid, Alan Freed, Benny Goodman, George Gershwin, Mezz Mezzrow, Al Jolson) had loved the black music of their day. The Beasties' demonstration of that love, however, takes on the same kind of well-meaning condescension that Lipsitz criticizes and that lies at the heart of Mailer's ideation of the middle-class white hipster as imaginary bad nigger out to raise some hell because that's where the juice is.

The Beasties appeared to wink and nod at what amounted to black stereotypes in order to show their allegiance to what they knew of black culture through hip-hop culture. From another perspective, however, and perhaps a more generous one, the gun-toting, fried chicken-eating, crack-smoking caricatures the Beasties drew of themselves may have served the same function as the nineteenth-century minstrel character Zip Coon, a buffoonish social misfit who offered a comic representation of black males but who was also a foil for white working-class criticism of upper-middle-class pretentiousness. The Beastie Boys' ghettoized high jinks threw a stink bomb into the living rooms of conservative white America and everybody who was hip enough got the joke. More important, perhaps, the Beasties successfully negotiated the problem of whiteness and black masculine desire that Tony Jefferson poses by appropriating the apparatus of hip-hop through music, language, dramatic street narratives, and body-ism, credibly (re)modeling it so that white males could now not simply aspire to be *with it*, but *be it*. The Beasties demonstrated not only formidable microphone and songwriting skills but a performance of swaggering black male deviance that they affected both as artifice and in the register of the real. White males may have been drawn in by the discourse of hardness in the post-Run-DMC new school rap game, but they were utterly incapable of living it until the Beastie Boys showed them a way into the culture, regardless of the fact that the experiential ground of being that they presumed to occupy was absurd on its face. White kids seemed not to notice, or simply not to care—the Beasties were the new personification of white hipness.

## Vanilla on Ice: The Limits of Wiggerism

Things would not go as well a few years later for Vanilla Ice, the first successful white solo rap performer and a two-hit wonder whose 1990 release *Ice*

*Ice Baby* became the first hip-hop song to hold the top spot on the *Billboard* Top 100 singles chart. The song's accompanying album *To the Extreme* was also a No. 1 hit on the *Billboard* 200 and rose to No. 6 on the R&B album chart. Within a matter of months Vanilla Ice was selling out concerts, signing lucrative deals, and publishing an autobiography, making him momentarily the biggest thing in pop music, certainly in hip-hop. It all effectively and abruptly ended, however, when he was accused of lying about his personal history, including being stabbed several times in a street fight, growing up in a tough black neighborhood, and coming up hanging out with gangbangers. Vanilla Ice's background seems to be at least partly a combination of truth and some perhaps boastful exaggeration. In his early childhood he lived in modest circumstances in a mixed Miami neighborhood, while his later teen years were spent as a well-off kid in an affluent suburb of Dallas. He was discovered by his manager Tommy Quon performing at a rough and tumble black nightclub in Dallas called City Lights, where he recruited his DJ, two bodyguards, and a crew of black dancers after his career took off. Vanilla Ice's connection to black life and music were real enough, but what appeared to be in dispute was the veracity of the 'hood tales that had been publicized about him during his years in Miami. In an interview he gave in 1991, after sustaining an extraordinary amount of media scrutiny and ridicule, Vanilla Ice tried to set the record straight on a number of personal details, but reasserted and affirmed his connection to the urban street and black life, telling James Bernard, an editor for *Source* magazine, that his "neighborhood was predominantly black, my school was predominantly black. I got 'go white boy, go white boy' from City Lights, a totally black club in Dallas. No other white person would set foot in that club, but I performed there every night. My black friends in seventh grade called me Vanilla. I got it from them."[23]

Like the Beastie Boys, Vanilla Ice was seen as highly marketable in the suburbs and expanded the audience for hip-hop among white suburban kids—*Ice Ice Baby* was played on radio stations that had ignored black music entirely. Whatever the truth of his private past, as a white male rapper in a predominantly black medium at a time when hardcore rap was entering the mainstream, Vanilla Ice perceived and understood the need to place himself within a context of the urban street, black masculinity, and socially deviant behavior in order to lend credibility to his machismo performance of self. As Bernard observed in the same article, "any rapper, but especially a white rapper, needs a 'street' credibility that Vanilla Ice's suburban upbringing doesn't automatically confer."[24]

Most of his debut album, however, is relatively free of gangsta-styled themes. On the single "Ice Ice Baby," he momentarily raps about gunplay and street exploits that seem no more farfetched, and in fact are far less contrived, than much of the braggadocio on the Beasties' *Licensed to Ill*. Vanilla Ice describes cruising in Miami with his friend Shay, who is packing a "gauge" (shotgun), while he is strapped with a "nine" (nine millimeter semi-automatic pistol). Arguably, any kind of bragging and boasting on record is allowable until one starts to boast about guns he doesn't own and crimes he didn't commit. Vanilla Ice describes a shootout where "gunshots ranged out like a bell/I grabbed my nine—All I heard were shells." He jumps in his car and tries to escape, worrying about getting carjacked. Meanwhile there are "Police on the scene, You know what I mean/They passed me up, confronted all the dope fiends," the implication being that because he is white, the police do not suspect him of being involved in the shootout and instead go after the (presumably) black dope fiends. That section aside, the rest of the songs on *To The Extreme* are innocuous G-rated raps about girls, partying, and having fun. Nonetheless, Vanilla Ice would not recover from the perception that he was a middle-class, suburban white kid who lied about his personal history to boost record sales, but what hurt him more was that he came off as "soft" and a poseur at a time when hardness and authenticity were becoming synonymous with masculinity and the black ghetto. Vanilla Ice's other problem was his totally cornball image, equal parts bubble-gum teenie-bopper idol and punked-out Captain America. His early look consisted of American flag–themed red, white, and blue outfits and a squared-off pompadour. It did not help that he appeared to have fashioned his image on that of M. C. Hammer (whom he toured with), another million-selling pop rap superstar who got no love in the 'hood.

In an attempt to revive his career and reinsert himself into the new political economy of hardcore street rap, Vanilla Ice subsequently retooled his image and tried to come off as thugged out, resurfacing in urban street wear and tattoos, and recording music with a much harder edge and more urban 'hood street narratives. In some of his later lyrics, he portrayed himself as a man who could commit cold-blooded murder. On his 1998 album *Hard To Swallow*, he takes on the persona of a hardcore gangster rapper in the song "Livin'," in which he imagines himself as a violent gangbanger, slitting the throats of his rivals and sitting on his roof peering through the telescope of a gun, but it was far too late for Ice to reinvent an image many had come to see as goofy. In the end he occasionally acquiesced in parodying himself, appearing on the television reality show *The Surreal Life* and Insane Clown Posse's *Juggalo Championship Wrestling*.

To be fair, Vanilla Ice's performance of white Negroism on *To The Extreme* was much less egregious than that of the Beastie Boys' *Licensed to Ill*.

Nonetheless, Vanilla Ice's fall from grace suggests how critical the sign of blackness and representations of urban street masculinity had become as new models of authenticity and credibility in a genre that was increasingly driven by narratives of street hustling, gun violence, and confrontations with police. Vanilla Ice's attempt to work a terrain of transvesting and gender performance based on deviance and gangsterism appeared to be inauthentic. His hardcore gangsta drag was too contrived and sophomoric to come off as anything more than parody. The actor Jamie Kennedy's comedic performance in the 2003 movie *Malibu's Most Wanted* by comparison was a more direct and therefore more honest parody of the white gangster wannabe who comes from a privileged background and who fetishes representations of hard black masculinity. Kennedy's satirical send-up of the gangsta lifestyle employs all the clichés—forty-ounce bottles of beer, hootchie mamas, casual violence, gunplay, and goofed-up street slang. The Beastie Boys were able to bring out the same kind of humor in a hip sort of way, but they never *pretended* to be real street thugs. Vanilla Ice tried to play it in the register of the real rather than as parody, at least that was the perception, and he only succeeded in making himself look silly.

## Whiteness and the New Masculine Desire

So much of what makes up the array of practices that constitute hip-hop culture is inscribed onto the body that to ignore the body would be to dismiss a good deal of what makes the culture so appealing. The body in hip-hop is in a perpetual state of animated signifying and social performance, so that "reading the body as a performing body requires viewing the body as a source of action and movement"[25] but also of situation or context, of drama and narrative, which means that real thugs with gangland tales to tell will always have the edge in commercial rap performance because the marketplace has created a demand for authenticity and realness over poseurs. Nonetheless, despite contestations around issues of agency, authenticity, cultural authorship, and exploitation, it should have come as no surprise that white youth who consume hip-hop music and identify with the culture would eventually begin to act out their own racial fantasies of black urban masculinity as social rebellion. In the white appropriation of hip-hop culture and style, however, *acting black* often and easily moves from the merely quaint to the predictably cliché, and from there to the absurdly grotesque.

John Seabrook, in his book *Nobrow: The Culture of Marketing, the Marketing of Culture*, updates Norman Mailer's hipster figure from the perspective of a young middle-class white male in the 1990s. He is walking down the street in New York City listening to the Notorious B.I.G.'s "Ready to Die," wearing "a black nylon convict-style cap,[26] a fashion I picked up from the homeys in the rap videos."[27] Later, riding the subway, he feels empowered because of the doo-rag, its association with black males and gangster criminality. Inspired by the music, he begins to imagine himself a menacing figure who lets "the gangsta style play down into my whiteboy identity, thinking to myself, 'Man you are the illest, you are sitting here on this subway and none of these people are going to FUCK with you, and if they do FUCK with you, you are going to FUCK them up. What's MY muthafuckin' name?'"[28] Seabrook articulates the allure of the hard man for young white males who gravitate to hardcore rap and who may make associations between the projection of masculine power through real or implied acts of violence as a means to acquire street credibility, respect, or personal self-empowerment. Although they are utterly incapable of living out these kinds of ubermasculine desires and fantasies in their own lives, these youth vicariously access such feelings through racialized commodity fetishism and the consumption of music, film, clothing, videos, computer games, and other parts of the apparatus of hardcore rap culture mediated through the mass media and the culture industry. In this new street theater of the racially absurd, the physical power, sexuality, and ability to inspire fear that black male bodies have historically conveyed become transferred onto white bodies in ways that usurp agency of the black body, exploits it as a site of social anxiety, and perpetuates its demonization. It is the emotional response to this spectacle that is most critical since feelings around blackness and masculinity embedded at the site of the body become complicit in the construction of unexamined fears and anxieties that perpetuate racial stereotypes and provide convenient justifications for ongoing racial prejudice, particularly against young black males.

Discourses around the black body in popular music and culture have nonetheless shifted considerably over the past few decades. The political currency of the black body in popular culture began to accrue in the 1960s and continued through the 1970s owing to a number of events, including the civil rights and black nationalism movements, the mainstreaming of soul music, and the cult popularity of so called blaxploitation films as well as the emergence of hip-hop culture. As I have discussed, these events recast black males in popular culture as powerful and alluring if also intimidating and dangerous, so that when hardcore rap entered the American mainstream in the 1980s and 1990s, black masculinities and the notion of hardness became the litmus test for a new ideal of cultural authenticity for young urban and suburban males.

Notions of implicit and explicit actors have now collapsed in on themselves so that the preference for mere poseurs has become passé. In performing representations of black masculinity whether on the stage or on the street, white hip-hop performers and consumers now aspire to an authenticity that, rather than attempting to obscure racial subtexts and the highjacking of black subjectivity, covets, foregrounds, and celebrates them. The rules of the new *keeping it real* game mean that credibility is everything, that credibility depends on authenticity, and that authenticity is bestowed on the mean streets of the black inner city. White anxiety around blackness has not historically diminished the racial desire attached to forms of black popular music and their cultural milieu, although as Leon Wynter writes, "the bar for authentic participation in the American experience that generates hip-hop culture is much higher than it was, say for white jazz musicians in the 1950s. The majority of the audience—the white majority—demands it. Where the old chain of white cultural appropriation has been broken, the role of whiteness in popular culture is fast being transformed."[29] Not only is whiteness being transformed through the appropriation of black expressive tropes in hip-hop culture, but youth from other races, cultures, ethnicities, and nationalities around the world are being transformed as well. Nonetheless, this type of exoticism has increasingly produced the kinds of racially reductive ghetto fantasies as Seabrook imagines, where black masculinities are only viewed and experienced at the level of the brute.

LL Cool J and Run-DMC were among the earliest rappers to focus attention on the black male body as a sign of masculine power and hypersexuality wedded as aggression and push back against society at large since they defied historical images of emasculation and subjugation. When LL Cool J ripped off his shirt to flaunt the taut muscled body once prized by slave traders and plantation owners, and Run-DMC mean-mugged *Rolling Stone* in black fedoras and the b-boy stance, they reinvented the buck/brute as the new and definitive representation of hip-hop maleness—young, aggressive, black, and urban—and sent the message to other adolescent males that to get down in this new culture they would have to step up. The emphatic posturing of young black males in hip-hop and hardcore rap culture would become indelible images in the American racial imagination, drawing "on decades of affectively invested, dominant cultural discourses and ideologies."[30] The subsequent "Afro-Americanization of white youth"[31] began with their adopting the sartorial style, language, and often the speech patterns of inner-city black youth, appropriating the affective gestures of blackness as the performance of the everyday. Only a handful of these youth have succeeded at the highest artistic and commercial levels of hip-hop music and rap performance even a quarter century after the music's creation since few have been able to convincingly meet the new threshold for blacking up and for the credible performance of black urban masculinity. Many of those who have attempted it and who have been successful have often done so by adopting models of black masculinity "represented as a pathological form of 'otherness'"[32] rather than as resistance to hegemonic racial oppression. Those who merely identify with the culture through consumption have learned to reproduce an affective quality of street-level performance that defines authenticity or *keeping it real* as keeping it ghetto.

In the 2007 VH1 reality/game show television series *The (White) Rapper Show*, white contestants vying for cash and a record deal portrayed themselves as real-life *wiggas* who mimicked and romanticized representations of inner-city black males, speaking in black slang, sporting tilted baseball caps, gold chains, and grillz, and fetishizing black rappers who came up on the street. In an episode where contestants competed to see who was the most "thugged out," the African American hardcore rapper Saigon made a cameo appearance to run down the basics of thugness, rattling off his time spent in prison, rolling with gangs, and committing criminal offenses like they were Boy Scout merit badges. Saigon reinserted the absent black male deviant presence into the series, reminding all poseurs that criminality was as critical in the rap game as microphone skills. The contestants then used "stolen" grocery store shopping carts to try and "catch a case" (getting charged with a crime), thrown from an abandoned apartment building, jacked bicycles with chain cutters, and traded vitriolic, black slang-laden *disses* with each other while cameras caught the action. The idiotic ideologies of racial acculturation and the frivolic attitude toward inner-city desperation that the show promoted to its supposedly hip audience only served as a reminder of how the circulation of pejorative representations of blacks in the 1800s brought about real political and social consequences for black folks over the next one hundred years and that culminated in the very ghettos they now romanticized as racial playground.

*The (White) Rapper Show* suggests how white notions of black subjectivity and the performance of black masculinities adopted by nonblack actors are not only often overwrought to the point of unintended parody and promote representations of blackness that are reductive and pejorative, but that may go largely unexamined because they are masked by whiteness, as it were. The ready accessibility and uncritical consumption of these kinds of images through what David Roediger has characterized as "the seeming intimacy of video culture" is further problematized since "the problems raised by corporate influences over deciding what is 'authentic' are great."[33] In hardcore rap themed music, video games, films, and other media, the performance of the real is reinserted back into the ground of the everyday as play, so that boundaries between performance and the real continue to shift and disintegrate.

This idea is captured remarkably well in the 1999 film *Whiteboyz*, in which a group of young white males in rural Iowa imagine themselves part of a community of black gangsters and thugs they learn to mimic from watching music videos of gangsta rap performers. The main protagonist, a naïve and guileless character who goes by the name Flip Dogg, confesses that he has never been to the ghetto, but opines, "I know what it's like." His overwrought use of black urban slang and mannerisms that he presumes all blacks share is disconcerting even to the one black friend he has. Flip Dogg and his friends embark on a misguided mission to Chicago's inner city where he hopes to make a drug deal, get paid, and live out his fantasies of a hustler's lifestyle. After a black friend agrees to introduce him to a gang of crack cocaine dealers (the film was apparently shot in Chicago's Cabrini-Green housing project using real gang members), Flip Dogg is quickly made out to be a cartoonish object of ridicule. He has brought less than $200 in cash with him and asks to be "fronted" with a load of cocaine on consignment because he fancies himself part of the community of black thugs and gangsters he has romanticized about. Even when he is attacked, robbed, and beaten by the gang members, he remains trapped in his illusionary world, oblivious to the severity of his situation. Thinking the beating is part of a gangland initiation ritual, he staggers to his feet and queries his assailants, "Am I in?"

Flip Dogg's contorted views of black culture are so ingrained that he literally has no other frame of reference. After getting into a shootout with the gang members, Flip Dogg and his friends flee back to Iowa disillusioned and humiliated. Victor Anderson's discussion of ontological blackness as "a type of categorical racial reasoning" or "a philosophy of racial consciousness"[34] illuminates how completely Flip Dogg has constructed his worldview around a view of blackness that is fantastical and illusory. Flip was raised on a farm by parents with little education or social status; his obsession with black culture leaves him even more socially isolated. Because of his family's financial troubles and low social standing, he has a sense of shared connection with underprivileged blacks that he understands and expresses in a rather perverted sort of way since his experiences with black males and black culture in general are largely limited to mediated images of black gangsters in music videos. Flip is somehow unable to distinguish between the performance of artifice and the performance of the real, having bought into the illusory world of hardcore "reality rap" and its allure of authenticity because many of its progenitors are people with whom he identifies with as the socially oppressed. Flip's racial reasoning, and the fact that he has had access to few black people in real life, lead him to take a reductionist and romanticized view of black life and culture that he believes he can become part of through emulating socially deviant behavior in language, dress, and deeds. The film is meant, of course, to critique exactly such reasoning by white adolescents drawn to hardcore styles of hip-hop.

## Eminem: The White Negro Gone Mad

The case of Eminem is more compelling and in some ways suggests why he has shown a great amount of endurance. Certainly he has a remarkable range of talent as a lyricist, but Eminem's origins as poor white trash growing up with a single mother, constantly on the move only to end up on the wrong side of Detroit's black/white, suburban/inner-city racial divide 8-Mile Road, also provided him with the kind of street credibility that the Beastie Boys, although respected by black lovers of hip-hop, never really earned the hard way, and that Vanilla Ice coveted perhaps a little too calculatedly. Eminem's portrayal of himself in the 2002 feature film *8-Mile* appears to be close to the truth of his early life, where he mixed socially with blacks and came up on the street in relative poverty, battle rapping in black clubs. His best friend in the film, Future, was modeled after rapper Proof, who was shot to death after shooting another man during a fight in an 8-Mile Road nightclub in 2006. Eminem spoke eloquently at Proof's funeral, saying, "without Proof, there would be no Eminem, no Slim Shady, and no D12," the Detroit-based rap collective formed by Proof. Eminem had been the only white member of D12, and it is where he first adopted the pseudonym Slim Shady.

After his rise to fame, Eminem signed D12 to his own Shady/Aftermath record label and toured with them until they too achieved fame. Unlike just about every white rapper before him, Eminem's performance of white Negroism was more real than poseur because his background and lived experience allowed him to negotiate the discourses of hardness and black masculinity that had been modeled to him on the street, but also by the Beastie Boys when he was a teenager. Not that he had ever claimed to run with gangs and deal drugs, and the over-the-top antics of the Beasties did not really fit his more complex and darker character. Nonetheless, he understood the new aesthetic of masculine hardness and its orientation to illicit street activities, violence, and deviant behavior, whether real or imagined, enough to know he needed to find where he could fit himself, and on his own terms. His maniacal alter ego Slim Shady was his solution to this dilemma. The Beastie Boys, Vanilla Ice, and Eminem may all "take their cues from a savage model,"[35] but Eminem, in his attempt to locate himself at the most extreme end of hardcore rap performance, began to dabble in ghoulish scenarios of murder, rape, and sadism from horrorcore[36] that even most black hardcore rappers avoid. Eminem's 1999 *The Slim Shady LP* brings together cartoonish representations of the brute and beast stereotypes taken past the reprehensible to the repulsive. Eminem's Slim Shady is the alienated white hipster turned Norman Bates, a mentally disturbed loser gone stark raving mad. The album's single "Just Don't Give a Fuck" plays with tropes of addiction and multiple personalities ("I'm doing acid, crack, smack, coke and smokin' dope then/My name is Marshall Mathers, I'm an alcoholic"), a summoning up of internalized demons as he traverses themes of violence, drugs, despair, bestiality, and derangement, declaring himself "half animal, half man, dumping your dead body inside of a fucking' trash can/with more holes than an Afghan." The song "'97 Bonnie and Clyde" depicts a macabre scene in which he murders his wife, stuffs her into the trunk of his car, and dumps her body off a pier. This song and others like it drew righteous indignation for its vile misogyny, which far exceeds the objectionable treatment of women depicted in much hardcore rap over the preceding decade. As Carl Rux observes in his essay "Eminem: The New White Negro": "Niggaz may talk bad about bitches and they baby's mama—Eminem brutally murders his."[37]

In the song "Guilty Conscience," Slim Shady eggs on three desperate men to commit a series of heinous crimes. He urges the first to rob a liquor store and shoot the store clerk ("Fuck that! Do that shit! Shoot that bitch!/Can you afford to blow this shit? Are you that rich?/Why you give a fuck if she dies?"). In another scene, he encourages a man to rape a drugged, underage girl ("Fuck this bitch right here on the spot bare/Til she passes out and she forgot how she got there"), and in the final scene, two shotgun blasts ring out at the end of the song as a betrayed husband kills his cheating wife and her lover in bed. Eminem's mentor and producer Dr. Dre makes a guest appearance on the song as his conscience, initially objecting to the slaughter, but finally approving it, presumably because the woman is guilty of having sex with another man, thus disrespecting him and undermining his masculinity. The song "I'm Shady," however, finds Eminem on the one hand in full psychotic rant but also self-reflexively critical, as if winking from behind his fool's mask to disavow his most offensive put-ons, not unlike the act of minstrel performers appearing on sheet music covers both with and without the burnt cork, reaffirming their whiteness and disavowing the tomfoolery of blackness. Eminem, on the other hand, never attempts to disavow blackness as much as he disavows whiteness. Like the Beastie Boys, Vanilla Ice, and a generation of young white male so-called wiggas, he chooses to inhabit ontological blackness as his own racialized comfort zone, but seeks the most extreme and profane interpretations of it from which to perform his version of the hypersexual, hypermasculine black brute.

A good deal of Eminem's success is owed to Dr. Dre, the pioneering West Coast gangsta rap producer who has orchestrated the music behind Eminem's other major work. Dr. Dre brought more than hard beats and gangsta credentials to the production, but adds racial value that further bolsters Eminem's street credibility much the same way that Def Jam, the first bona fide hip-hop record label, added juice to the Beastie Boys' *Licensed to Ill.* Vanilla Ice, by comparison, did not have this kind of muscle catching his back. Dr. Dre's presence animates the absent black presence in Eminem's music, not in the abstract way in which Elvis channeled blackness through his own whiteness, but in a tangible way that allowed Eminem to establish credibility with black audiences as few white performers before him had achieved.

The use of incendiary words over the course of Eminem's albums may be viewed in a somewhat different light than when used by socio-politically savvy comedians or by black hardcore rappers. On the one hand, they are deliberately provocative but often pointlessly gratuitous; he is not attempting to push the limits of free speech or challenge Victorian morality even though he may have grown up using such language among peers. Incendiary language is critical to the apparatus he is constructing, which, like horror films and horrorcore, rests on the shock value inherent in portraying something horrific that is likely to repulse, offend, and titillate. On the other hand, the use of language that appropriates working-class black vernacular folk idioms and urban street slang has become fashionable for white teens who aspire to urban hipness by engaging the apparatus of hardcore hip-hop culture. James Toback's 1999 film *Black and White*, which follows a group of class privileged but disaffected white teenagers who befriend a group of young black gangsters from Harlem, offers some interesting if simplified observations in this regard. The film, which features Mike Tyson, Robert Downey Jr., and several members of the Wu-Tan Clan, never makes much of a point in the end although it tries to suggest some very real reasons why white kids who feel alienated from their wealthy but straight-laced backgrounds would find attraction in identifying with hard-edged young black gangsters they perceive as cool and who can provide them with drugs, emotional excitement, and sex. They use black slang and take on the mores and mannerisms of the thugs they hang out with. Rap music, black-inflected speech and language use, and a rejection of middle-class whiteness give them a sense of their own hipness and a kind of affective empowerment wherein they can see themselves as more black than white. Their association with this group of black men essentially gives them a "ghetto pass" into a closed, dangerous, and exotic community that most white kids only get to visit on records and music videos, although they all "identify with violence, scatology, and sexism in rap rather than with black music and culture"[38] in broader terms. The teens in *Black and White* engage in their own racial carnivalesque where they are free to opt out of whiteness and the pretentious dictates of upper-middle-class privilege (a teenage girl gives her nagging corporate executive father a lecture on the difference between the terms *nigger* and *nigga*), but there is always the sense that they know they are in a world in which they only tenuously inhabit, that it is playful fantasy.

In Eminem's case, his *relationality* to black music carries the weight of authenticity not just because of Dr. Dre's beats, but because he grew up in a multiracial urban street milieu where hip-hop culture and rap music were part of the fabric of his own life. Like Elvis, Eminem has an acknowledged gift for replicating a black music style that grew from a genuine intimacy with black people, although the performance of that gift has more often involved acting out the most egregious caricatures of black male deviancy. In Elvis' case, this amounted to exaggerating the suggestion of sexual transgression, while Eminem invokes the post-Reconstruction trope of the black beast through horrific scenarios of sadistic violence. In either case, both of them assume subjectivities that play on hundreds of years of white fear and anxiety around the black male body.

Although Eminem collapses the notion of explicit and implicit actors that Elvis merely inverts, he nonetheless engages the idea of masking by employing an alter-ego that is revealing. While the use of *shady* suggests undertones of race and the idea of moral ambivalence, the term *slim* has been used as a moniker for any number of larger than life black males, from the guitarists Guitar Slim and Memphis Slim to Iceberg Slim, the legendary street hustler, pimp, and bad man who toward the end of his life wrote novels about the seedy underworld of vice and crime. Rather than paying homage to Iceberg Slim by signifying on his first name as many hardcore-styled rappers, including Ice-T, Ice Cube, Vanilla Ice, Doctor Ice, Mr. Ice, and Kid Frost have done (no doubt to suggest the coldness that lies at the heart of the hard man persona), Eminem slyly plays on the less well worn second name Slim, inventing by the addition of the name Shady, a darkly evil persona that is even more cold and cruel than the characters Iceberg Slim portrayed in his novels. Slim Shady reflects Eminem's appropriation of black male subjectivity to construct an identity that is part musical hero and part deviant social actor. This carnivalesque of racial masking becomes Eminem's way of not just working through his personal struggles, disappointments, and demons, but of channeling his own interpretation of white narratives of black male deviance, moral degeneracy, and criminal-minded sociopathology.

On his second album, *The Marshall Mathers LP*, Eminem again plays with his multiple personality roles and removes the mask to reveal explicit and implicit actors Eminem and Slim Shady as one Marshall Mathers. In the song "The Way I Am," as he critically dissects his own fame and hypervisibility, he appears to opt out of whiteness by criticizing "cocky Caucasians who think I'm some wigger who just tries to be black cause I talk with an accent/and grab on my balls, so they always keep asking the same fuckin questions, 'What school did I go to, what 'hood I grew up in'/The why, the who what when, the where, and the how." Eminem defends his ontological blackness as a manifestation of the way he is in the register of the real. By dealing with this issue openly on record, he also fends off the kinds of questions intended to check the veracity of his 'hood credentials that ensnarled Vanilla Ice.

Eminem often underscored the connection to the horror genre by appearing with such affectations as a hockey mask and a chainsaw. In live concerts he often used a large knife to slice up a life-sized, rubber effigy of his estranged wife. These are obvious references to slasher films like *Psycho* and *Halloween*, but in them, Eminem also (re)interprets his maniacal appropriations of the nylon stock cap-wearing, razor blade-toting, black male as social monster. In "Kill You," Eminem iterates a similar theme of personal power that is part maniacal revenge fantasy when he intones, "you don't wanna fuck with Shady, 'cause Shady will fucking kill you." Invoking the threat of physical violence and chaos that Norman Mailer rhapsodizes in *The White Negro* have been a fixture in white performance of black masculinities certainly since minstrelsy. Eminem, the Beastie Boys, and Vanilla Ice all follow the same equation, that authenticity in the performance of black masculinity finds it necessary to invoke themes of deviance and violence.

For his 2002 record *The Eminem Show*, however, Eminem displays a much broader diversity of thematic material that puts some distance between Eminem the entertainer and Slim Shady the monster, and reveals more of himself as Marshall Mathers. In the song "White America" he directly confronts issues around race and the fact of his own whiteness, recognizing that it has been both a curse and a blessing. When he was trying to break into the business, "no one gave a fuck, I was white/No labels wanted to sign me, almost gave up, I was like 'fuck it.' Until I met Dre, the only one who looked past [his whiteness], gave me a chance/and I lit a fire up under his ass." On the other hand, Eminem recognizes that because of his whiteness, he has sold more records than if he had been black, and that he has expanded the audience for rap among white suburban adolescents who were into West Coast hardcore, noting how "kids flipped when they found out I was produced by Dre/that's all it took, and they were instantly hooked right in/and they connected with me too because I looked like them." He suggests that his whiteness has caused him to be subjected to even more scrutiny since he is popularizing to white kids a kind of black music that no doubt horrifies their parents. He also drags into the open white fears of miscegenation that had been at the heart of attacks on 1950s rock 'n' roll when he rhymes, "surely hip-hop is never a problem in Harlem, only in Boston, after it bothered the fathers of daughters starting to blossom." In instances like this and in several other songs over the course of his albums, Eminem appears to want to shift from his usual pathological bad nigger impersonation and become something of the heroic bad man, pointing out the hypocrisy of adults, the reality of racism, and the paradox of his success in appealing to a primarily white audience by performing an uncompromisingly black music.

After releasing the somewhat retrospective album *Encore* in 2004, retiring from performing for several years, and undergoing drug rehabilitation, Eminem appeared to be sending a message that he was rethinking himself and the nature of his music, and that he might kill off the homicidal Slim Shady; in a skit at the end of *Encore*, Slim Shady is heard apparently being shot. In 2009, however, he came back seemingly with a vengeance when he released *Relapse*, a record that contains perhaps his most horrific scenarios of drug-induced violence and schizophrenic brutality. The record opens with a nightmare in which the Slim Shady character is revived (in slasher films the killer is always dispatched in the end only to be revived for a bloody encore) before launching into the ghoulish "3 a.m.," narrated by a psychopathic, drug-crazed serial killer who rhymes "I cut and I slash, slice, and gash, last night was a blast/I can't quite remember when I had that much fun off of a half pint of the Jack." On the song "Insane" the narrator recounts being molested by his stepfather and describes sexual acts of astonishing lewdness ("Fuck 'em in the ass, suck the cum out while you're belching/Burp belch and go back for a second helping") that revive his roots in horrorcore. In the end, Eminem's interpretation of the hard man appears based not on psychic and emotional invulnerability to pain but just the opposite, an extreme vulnerability, his own emotional torment and an admitted addiction to drugs that finally overwhelm him to the point that he becomes a psychotic sociopath. In the end, Eminem is guilty of the same kind of brutal equation that fueled the 'hood fantasies of the Beasties and Vanilla Ice, all of whom invoke the subtext of racial transgression and the imagery of the brute in order to stroke anxiety among white adults and glee among adolescent white males.

All three performers ultimately suggest how the complexities of racial intercourse and interaction in the post-hip-hop racial environment are more contradictory than those of the past because they occur in a "post-racist"[39] environment. By this, Richard Thompson Ford does not mean to suggest that racism is a thing of the past, but that it implies a new stage of racial behavior in which certain ideas and practices remain pervasive, but expressed in different ways. The post-racist consumer of hardcore hip-hop unabashedly indulges the stereotypes of the black thug, the pimp, the drug dealer, the crack whore, and the hustler, "free to be explicitly and crudely bigoted because he does so with tongue planted firmly in cheek."[40] It is, as he suggests, racism without racists since there may be no racist intent per se in such representations, but the acting out of reductionist racial fantasies merely becomes "the continuation of racism by other means."[41] Nonetheless, romantically mistaking white consumers of hip-hop as a vanguard of antiracist social change need not reject the incontestably diverse nature of American hybridity or of contemporary hip-hop culture. The requirements of the new authenticity collapse notions of implicit and explicit racial actors either in the true spirit of revolutionary racial politics or because the new Negroism demands it. In any case, what is perhaps needed, as Lipsitz has argued, are more ethical models for racial border crossings that challenge in positive ways and that are progressive rather than regressive, and that are empowering rather than exploitative.

## Brother Ali's Radical Black Subjectivity

The most important thing about Minneapolis-based rapper Brother Ali is not how he looks, and yet, it is understandably the first thing one pays attention to upon seeing him for the first time. Looking at him tends to expose how the socially constructed nature of race and the black/white bifurcation that still largely defines it in the United States—what sociologist and historian W. E. B. DuBois famously characterized as "the color line"—are more complex than even we assume. Ali is intriguing and compelling on a number of levels. Born to middle-class parents in Wisconsin, he moved to East Lansing when he was a child, but his Midwest upbringing was anything but normal. Ali presents a rather self-effacing persona, a demeanor perhaps tempered by his devout adherence to classical Islam, which he studied in Singapore, learning Arabic so that he could read the Holy Quran in its original language. He converted to the religion after reading *The Autobiography of Malcolm X* when he was fifteen years old. Ali's construction of self, his speech patterns, language, and body-ism, reference black urban masculinity—he appears to be a light-skinned African American male, and many people took him for that in the early part of his career. He largely dispenses with fashion, preferring inexpensive sneakers, jeans, and T-shirts—workingman's clothes—but he affects an air of gravitas that commands respect. He is a big man, but onstage he seems bigger. Offstage, the macho swaggering and prerequisite bragga-docio of the rap performer fades, and he can come off as reserved, even shy.

What makes Brother Ali compelling in terms of race and hybridity is his albinism, a rare condition caused by a lack of pigmentation in the skin; his facial hair is white and his eyes appear pinkish. Because of this condition, he occupies a racial borderland between black and white that has made all the difference in terms of the path he has traveled in life. The question of his race and his albinism are subjects he did not often address publicly until fairly recently because he feels these things often overshadow his music, and yet they are the things that make his music possible and that make him who he uniquely is. After meeting him at a performance in Seattle in 2003 shortly after the release of his first Rhymesayers CD *Shadows on the Sun,* we subse-quently had a frank and candid conversation in which he opened up about his racial heritage, his past and his life experiences, something he rarely did at the time. Since then he has become more open about these things in the few media interviews he gives. At the time of our conversation, he admitted to deliberately choosing to remain ambiguous about his race. "I don't tell people what my parents are," he told me. "I don't tell these interviewers and kids that buy my records. I don't tell them that just because of the fact they have a hard time thinking out of 'are you black or are you white?' and don't understand how much cultural it really is, and how much spiritual it really is, and how much of these other things really make up what race is, more than ethnicity does. Race is a lot more cultural than what people want to realize."[42]

Ali began to inhabit the paradigm of ontological blackness when, because of his albinism and the fact that he looked different, a racialized Other alienated from whiteness, he was ostracized and often took vicious beatings from the white kids he grew up with, harrowing incidents he recalls on such songs as "Picket Fence" and "Win Some, Lose Some." At some point in his childhood he was befriended by a black kid and spent nights at his home. On Sunday mornings he was obligated to attend church with the family. Through these interactions Ali developed a deep and genuine appreciation of black worship and social life. As he gradually developed an orientation to black culture and became interested in hip-hop, he made other black friends and began to inhabit a space of black subjectivity, rejecting a whiteness he felt had rejected him. "I used to be very anti-white," recalled during our conversation. "I used to be very much angry. For a long time I was so mad and so angry, and so borderline hateful towards white people because I experienced not being fully white, but at the same time my parents were white, and I know that even my face—I had this European nose, and just hating that. There was some self-hate involved there for a while. For me it was a very touchy mixture."

Ali's rejection of whiteness and his construction of an ontological black subjectivity was the way in which he began to accept himself and find healing, though he admits that for some time it led to him having to deal with major identity issues. As he recalled: "I used to really be confused, man. At that time I straight up was like 'I'm black,' you know what I mean? And it was an older guy that explained to me how that wasn't true. For a long time I was like, 'I'm not white. White people are terrible. I'm black,' and I still in ways might feel that way. I still think of myself more so as a black person than a white person, but I know better than that now. Black people understand, more than anybody on this earth, the feeling of powerlessness, so anybody else that has experienced that at all certainly has a partner there."

One of the earliest rap albums to catch his attention was Boogie Down Productions' *Criminal Minded*. He developed a fascination for KRS-ONE after the rapper helped to sponsor the Stop the Violence Movement in the 1980s.[43] He recalled that "KRS-ONE became the most influential person in my life, and he probably was that for a good five years just because he just blew my mind, just to be that powerful and intense and intelligent like that, bringing up things I had never been exposed to before like the history of Africa, white supremacy, the history of Europe." When he was about twelve, he remembers going to hear KRS-ONE give a lecture in East Lansing and said, "When I left there, I wanted to be *him*, you know?" Ali immersed himself in the study of black literature and biographical works, and found other rappers he admired and respected like Chuck D, Heavy D, and Big Daddy Kane, men who had never graduated from college, but whom he considered had the street-level savvy and mother wit he calls "hard-core smart." His relationship with his family of origin he recalls as "very rocky," and his music is filled with autobiographical references that trace a path of personal self-development and gradual empowerment that he attributes to his interaction with black people and culture. He confided in our discussion that "basically, all of the real-life lessons in my life for the most part I learned from, all of the mentors in my life have always been black people. Always."

Ali does a fair amount of macho posturing and braggadocio while dissing rival rappers, but unlike Vanilla Ice or Eminem, he is not trying to construct himself as another white Negro as bad nigger. More often than not he takes the posture of the bad man, one that finds his most powerful songs engaging progressive social and political themes. He sees his life and his music as prophetic, of bearing witness to the sufferings of the weak and the dispossessed, and grounded in the personal strength he has drawn from black religious faith, his devotion to Islam, and his struggle to hold on to his humanity in the face of the discrimination he has experienced because of his physical features. The racial border region between blackness and whiteness that he occupies and the sense of marginalization he has experienced as a result of it have become spaces from which to speak truth to power, to interrogate racism and other categories of intolerance and exclusion while inviting us to transcend them. At other times Ali exposes "the invisibility and normative position that whiteness holds" in American life in a way that makes "whiteness visible to whites—exposing the discourses, the social and cultural practices, and the material conditions that cloak whiteness and hide its dominating effects."[44]

White supremacist ideology, intolerance, racism, the legacy of slavery, personal disillusionment, domestic abuse, and his struggles for identity and community were central themes he addressed in unsparing terms on *Shadows on the Sun,* which lends insight into a tortured childhood that shaped his social and racial views as well as his artistic vision. The song "Picket Fence" is typically autobiographical, recounting a rite of passage from innocence to self-awareness and a journey of self-discovery that is both painful and transformative. With the strains of what sounds like a black spiritual humming in the background, Ali describes an early idyllic childhood "living out life behind a picket fence/Happy go lucky scared of no one," before "blight and white supremacy heisted my innocence." One of the prime metaphors for the American Dream, certainly, is that of the white picket fence that symbolizes the prosperity that many enjoyed in the United States during the postwar years, particularly middle-class white suburbanites. Here it becomes a metaphor for youthful innocence and its defilement. Childhood cruelty visited upon him by classmates made him aware of his albinism, whiteness and his estrangement from it. As he recounts, "then came the laughter, and outside I'm battered/Picket fence shattered/I saw myself as a bastard tagalong, harassed and spat up/By the children of slave masters who passed it on." His childhood tormentors caused him to fall "face first into self-hate," where "every mirror that I saw back then had the earth's ugliest human being in it." Ali's experiences of being taunted and beaten ("they would kick me until they got tired or I act dead,") are reminiscent of any number of accounts of racial brutality suffered by blacks at the hands of white racists and segregationists particularly in the American South from slavery and Reconstruction through the civil rights movement of the 1950s and 1960s. What amounted to racial violence would forever inform Ali's perceptions about race and identity and help instill in him a deep abhorrence of racial bigotry and social injustice.

His moment of transformation and redemption comes later in the song, where, as he writes, he is approached on the playground by an elderly black woman, "the old sister who hums gospel tunes" (her presence palpable in the humming that we hear beneath his rhymes), who delivers a message of hope and personal salvation, telling him, "You look the way you do because you're special, not the short bus way, I mean that God's gonna test you." The experience gave him a feeling of being somehow anointed rather than deformed, which he voices in the further lines attributed to the woman who approaches him: "And all of this pain is training for the day when you will have to lead with the gift God gave to you/Grown folks don't see it but the babies do/And there's a chance that you can save a few/And time will prove that, she started my movement/She didn't tell me to take it, she told me to use it." In relating the incident during our talk, he recalls this time in his life: "Ever since I was a young kid I've had this feeling like not being part of white America, you know, not feeling like I had the benefit of that, not feeling membership in that and not feeling togetherness with that, and basically feeling that togetherness with black people, always feeling comfortable with black people, always feeling I could be myself, always feeling like people related to me as a person, understood me, that I understood them, always just feeling comfortable, and then I've always just liked black culture better, and because of that I've always benefited more from black wisdom."

As a result of this and other experiences in his life, Ali has come to read his albinism as a kind of higher calling, and a form of revolutionary, radical black subjectivity that characterizes the spirit of social progressiveness and political activism of African Americans in the twentieth century. In *Yearning: Race, Gender and Cultural Politics,* bell hooks formulates the idea of radical black subjectivity as a way to move beyond merely resisting the discourse of white supremacy and marginalization to a position of self-empowerment and progressive social change. Its challenge is to move beyond the rhetoric of victimization to one that sees marginalization as a site of resistance. hooks names marginality "as a site of transformation where liberatory black subjectivity can fully emerge," and emphasizes that there is a "definite distinction between that marginality which is imposed by oppressive structure and that marginality one chooses as site of resistance, as location of radical openness and possibility."[45] Brother Ali's journey from marginalization to self-discovery caused him to reject a whiteness that had rejected him, and to adopt ontological blackness as a way to heal and empower himself and construct a progressive body of music that powerfully speaks from the racial borderland marked by his albinism. In that space, the space of a marginalized Other who complicates the black/white binary, Ali has constructed for himself the kind of identity that hooks envisioned, one that "emerges from

the meeting of diverse epistemologies, habits of being, concrete class location, and radical political commitments" and that in the end, moves beyond
an identity "informed by a narrow cultural nationalism marking continued
fascination with the power of the white hegemonic other."[46]

Ali's ontological blackness embraces not simply the historic struggles
against racism and its injustices but the contemporary possibilities of social
change through private protest and public activism, rather than playing to
reductive representations and appropriations of blackness. He sees himself as
much a preacher as an entertainer, ministering to and leading a congregation
of like-minded people in a movement of conscience toward community and
social justice. He expresses consternation at the fact that some young white
hip-hop fans gravitate to him for reasons he considers border on cultural
racism. As he put it during our discussion: "In the underground there is an
almost all majority white movement where a lot of the artists are white, a lot
of the fans are white. You got fans who have no black friends, who have no
connection to black culture whatsoever who like these white underground
hip-hop groups, and to them that's better, and they feel like it's superior cre-
atively. They feel like it's intellectually superior, like it's more complex. They
feel like it's all around better hip-hop than 50 Cent." Nonetheless, he is able to
craft teachable moments from these interactions. As he related, "sometimes
with them (white fans) their problem already is that they can only relate to
somebody that looks like them, so I feel like if I let them have that about me
sometimes, like 'alright, y'all want to relate to me? We're not the same, but if
y'all want to feel like we're the same for a minute to have to learn from me,
I'll do that.' That's OK."

Several songs from *Shadows on the Sun* testify to Ali's visionary socio-
musical movement. Perhaps the most bleak and powerful of these is "Room
With a View," which speaks to the blight of inner-city poverty and desperation. The song engages themes common to hardcore styles of rap such as
casual violence, drug dealing, poverty, prostitution, and gangland drive-by
shootings, but not in a gratuitous or opportunistic manner. Despite being
raised in relative middle-class comfort, he has spent much of his adult life
in a working-class struggle for survival (he left home and married when he
was seventeen) while trying to keep his artistic dreams alive, knowing home-
lessness and poverty, working odd jobs to support a wife and child. There
is no ghetto glory or 'hood heroism in Ali's rendering of the street, only the
casualties and catastrophes of the misfortunate. His reading of ghetto life
is unrelenting in exposing the never-ending tragedies of hopelessness that
focuses less on the players—the hustlers, gangstas and thugs—and more

on ordinary people who are victims of their circumstances. In the world he describes from the window of his Minneapolis apartment, "slinging crack is not seen as a fucking recreation but a vocation." In Ali's urban reality, parents only touch their children when a whip is brought out, where "we don't have Bar Mitzvah's/we become men the first time our father hits us." In Ali's 'hood, "Sister Regina from across the street is beautiful/but for fifty bucks ain't nothing she won't do to you." It is a world where "hoop dreamers" eventually become disillusioned, "pain strangles them from within, 'til the belt around the arm makes the veins stand at attention." The song is more reminiscent of the kind of indignation and social consciousness expressed in songs like Grandmaster Flash and the Furious Five's "The Message" or Run-DMC's "It's Like That" than in many of the nihilist street narratives of the gangsta and the thug that offer mere rage without moral counterpoint.

Ali's "Forest Whitaker," a tribute of sorts to the Academy Award–winning African American actor, deals with overcoming the prejudices associated with personal appearance. It testifies to Ali's personal transformation and self acceptance, and alludes to Whitaker's having succeeded in an occupation with fairly narrow norms of beauty, where the Hollywood "leading man" has historically celebrated dashing white males. "Whitaker" finds Ali on the other side of his struggle about his own physical features, his self-confidence intact, drawing strength from a successful black male who beat the odds when race and appearance should have been overwhelmingly against him. He comes to terms with his condition when he writes, "I'm albino man, I know I'm pink and pale/And I'm hairy as hell, everywhere but fingernails," but having moved far from the depression and self-hatred he confesses in "Picket Fence," he has now found a measure of real peace reflected in the lines "You might think I'm depressed as can be/But when I look in the mirror I see sexy ass me." He ministers to those who have felt the sting of discrimination based on looks with a final shout out and makes a powerful statement of self-love and acceptance when he rhymes, "To everyone out there who's a little different/I say damn a magazine, these are God's fingerprints/You can call me ugly but can't take nothing from me/I am what I am doctor, you ain't gotta love me." He confirmed these feelings during our conversation, acknowledging that "I know that being albino is the main part of it, the main part of why I think I ended up being the way that I am and why I've made the choices that I've made before I even realized that I was necessarily making those choices."

Ali makes perhaps his most profound statement around personal identity, whiteness, and radical black subjectivity in the song "Daylight," from the 2007 album *The Undisputed Truth*, where he takes on the question of his racial identity that has been so constant in his life by proclaiming "Race is a made up thing I don't believe in it/My genes tie me to those that despised me, made a living killing the ones that inspired me." Here Ali openly interrogates the social construction of race while also acknowledging a biological heritage he rejects because of its legacy of white supremacy and slavery. He also distances himself from wanting to be seen as merely an entertainer and again reaffirms the visionary and revolutionary aspect of his art when he rhymes "I ain't just talking about singing and dancing, I was taught life and manhood by black men/So I'm a product of that understanding/And a small part of me feels like I am them." This lyric speaks perhaps most honestly and plainly to Ali's performance of a radical black masculine subjectivity, and the enduring influence it has had in shaping his own self-identity and social convictions.

Ali directly challenges his white fans into self-reflection on issues around race and social justice. The message in "Daylight" is similar to Eminem's "White America," but is more clearly rendered in unambiguous and defiant terms when he protests that "I don't want the white folks that praise me to think they can claim me 'cause you didn't make me/You don't appreciate what I know to be great yet you relate to me." Like Eminem, Vanilla Ice, and the Beastie Boys, Brother Ali has brought white fans into hip-hop and rap music, but he appears to understand better than any of them the burdens, challenges, and perhaps responsibility that comes with appropriating a cultural expression created by marginalized and oppressed minority youth. He challenges the notion of fan loyalty based primarily on shared whiteness, something "that frustrates me and what can I say/'cause I know that I benefit from something I hate." Yet, he offers something of an olive branch and an invitation, a challenge perhaps, for like-minded individuals to join his dedication to racial and social justice when he tells his fans "make no mistake our connection ain't fake/It's never too late to clear off the slate." By making it clear that he rejects fans who relate to him only because he is white, he is not allowing them to casually invest in the "post-racial" consumption of a black cultural product without reflecting on the historical and contemporary consequences of American racial oppression.

Ali's song "Uncle Sam Goddamn" also from *The Undisputed Truth*, is even more direct and unsparing in its assault on racial bigotry and the history of American slavery. An homage to Nina Simone's civil rights era protest song "Mississippi Goddamn," Ali critiques "the world's most despicable slavery trade/Pioneered so many ways to degrade a human being that it can't be changed to this day/Legacy so ingrained in the way that we think we no longer need chains to be slaves/Lord it's a shameful display." The video for the song depicts images of slave ships, lynchings, Ku Klux Klan rallies, civil rights era protests, student riots, war carnage, and flag-draped caskets of fallen soldiers from Iraq. The chorus intones: "Welcome to the United Snakes/Land of the thief home of the slave/The grand imperial guard where the dollar is sacred and power is God." The song also takes on U.S. imperialism and caused Ali to lose a lucrative tour sponsorship when he refused to edit out material that criticized an American military-industrial war machine that has often targeted people of color. Ali offers a compelling critique of such interventions, their justifications aside, when he rhymes: "Talking 'bout you don't support a crackhead/What you think happens to the money from yo' taxes/Shit the government an addict/With a billion dollar a week kill brown people habit."

Ali's vision seems to reach full maturity with his 2009 CD simply entitled *US*, which finds a point of racial conciliation. The material is less embattled than his previous work, his personal life having found a measure of peace and comfort and a unified message of hope for human reconciliation that reaches out across lines of race, class, ethnicity, and religious divisions. In the title single "US" he delivers a message to all of his fans that "to me all ya'll look exactly the same/Fear faith compassion and pain." The song may be as close as Ali has come to preaching a Sunday sermon (he later rhymes "Street preacher is what a fan once called me/I been called worse and tried to live up"), delivering the anti-racist message that "try as we may to mask it remains such as your religion or your past and your race, the same color blood just pass through our veins and tears taste the same when they're splashing your face." With "US," Ali appears to have moved beyond merely rejecting whiteness and its history and makes a plea beyond the things that divide, reaching out with the lines that the world "is getting too small to stand in one place/It's like roommates just sharing one space." His message is finally forward looking and optimistic as well as conciliatory when he delivers the lines "Can't separate and still carry the weight/gotta heal get away from the fear and the hate/gotta shake free from the chains, you see what remains/just a human being end of the day." In the final strains, he seems to come full circle from the ruptures of his earlier life, finding redemption and salvation in his own life, but like a benevolent bodhisattva, or echoing the sermons of Dr. Martin Luther King Jr., also wishing redemption for others, proclaiming that "can't nobody be free unless we're all free/there's no me and no you it's just us."

Brother Ali's performance of non-exploitative representations of black subjectivity offers, as Annalee Newitz and Matt Wray suggest in *White Trash: Race and Class in America,* "one model for reconceiving whiteness within the evolving political project of multiculturalism" that could help to effect the kinds of work around racial self-recognition and self-consciousness raising that have been largely absent in racial discourses dominated by whiteness. The kinds of borderline racialized identities that Brother Ali articulates, although not unproblematic, nonetheless bespeak "certain commonalities between oppressed whites and oppressed racial groups."[47] Like white trash discourse, Brother Ali uses his otherness to construct music that "speaks to the hybrid and multiple nature of identities" and the ways in which American hybridity is often formed and shaped by contradictory and conflicting relations of social power.[48] Brother Ali represents something perhaps unique in hip-hop culture as a white rap artist (he resists the tag "white rapper," fully aware of the negative baggage attached to the term) who has translated what Cornel West characterizes as "niggerization"[49] into an alternative and credible expression that is anti-racist, anti-misogynistic, non-exploitive, and anti-materialistic and who has drawn critical praise for his music as well as respect from other rappers for not compromising his values in order to achieve mainstream commercial success.

In the end, Ali eschews the nihilistic caricature of the bad nigger in favor of the socially conscious and morally committed heroism of the bad man who lives not just for self, but for others in his community. Brother Ali's performance of radical black subjectivity and black masculinity not only repudiates hundreds of years of condescending and paternalistic appropriations of black subjectivity, but challenges white consumers of black culture to seek more ethical ways of engagement with black people and black life. To paraphrase the words of Audre Lorde, Ali's radical black subjectivity can be defined in terms of an oppositional worldview, a consciousness, an identity, a standpoint that exists not only as that struggle that also opposes demonization but as that movement that enables creative, expansive self-actualization. Ali's radical black subjectivity is finally defined in terms of inclusion rather than exclusion, rendered in music and personal performance that offers a compelling alternative to the commodified gangstas and thugs of hardcore hip-hop that the culture industry routinely offers as contemporary models of masculine performance and desire.

One could argue that Ali perhaps pushes hooks' suggestion that there needs to be more space for "fluid notions of black identity" and "marginal perspectives"[50] a little far, an argument she raises herself when she discusses frustrating confrontations with "the white avant-garde in politically charged cultural contexts in which they seek to appropriate and usurp radical efforts to subvert static notions of black identity."[51] It is a legitimate charge that such appropriations happen again and again, and recalls Ingrid Monson's eloquent criticism of white hipness. Nonetheless, if we may return to the ruminations of George Lipsitz, the case can be made that such appropriations need not exist solely as "new aesthetic and political directions white folks might move in,"[52] as hooks sees it. Nearly two hundred years separate Jim Crow from Vanilla Ice, *The (White) Rapper Show,* Eminem, the Beastie Boys, and a legion of other wanksta wiggers. There is no reason to believe that such appropriations will cease. If it were the case however, that African American culture might come to be seen as, in Michele Wallace's critical view, "the starting point for white self-criticism"[53] rather than continuing to function as merely a funhouse of racial play, I think it might be fair to ask, what's so bad about that?

# Epilogue

Hip-hop is as popular among youth in Europe as it is in many parts of the world and has had an active if relatively small underground scene since the early 1980s. Masculine performance by adolescent and young white males in the culture of hip-hop in much of Europe derives from interpretations of American black masculinity modeled via electronically mediated sources that are now readily available, as are live performances by top name African American rap acts who have been touring West, Central, and Eastern Europe for the past twenty or thirty years. Such appropriations are not as central to the formation of masculine identity for European young males as they are in the United States, but where they are, they typically occur in the absence of any real information or context regarding African American life and culture. Styles of clothing, adornment, and the manner in which they are worn are often the most obvious signs of an affective investment in fetishized notions of masculinity as seen through the lens of inner-city gang culture in the United States, even though street-level gangs, drug-related violent crime, and incidents of gun violence in European countries are small by comparison.

In 2007, I attended a concert by 50 Cent in the Czech Republic capital of Prague that had been heavily advertised for several weeks with a darkened, grimacing image of the Queens, New York, rapper on large posters throughout the city. I was admittedly more curious to see who buys enough tickets to a 50 Cent concert to sell out a medium-sized arena in this stately old Central European capital where a large portion of the inhabitants still do not speak English. Black rappers are certainly well known in this part of the world (Tupac Shakur is very popular in Warsaw, where T-shirts with his image can readily be found in mainstream retail outlets; at a popular family-oriented

Turkish bath house in Budapest, I bumped into a young man who had "Thug Life" tattooed across his back) and deeply admired by young Eastern European males who follow the music. The crowd in Prague was quite diverse by age and gender but as racially monolithic as the city appears on most days. Scanning the crowd for the two hours of the performance, I could not find another black person in the arena other than the ones on stage. There were kids there who looked as young as six, some hoisted onto the shoulders of their parents, making it a family event, indeed, one of the most highly anticipated pop music shows to come to Prague in the year that I was there. The bigger part of the audience standing on the floor appeared to be adolescent teenage boys, thugged out in gangsta style—baggy pants, sports jerseys, tilted baseball caps, expensive sneakers, a few earrings, and oversized gold chains hanging down their chests. It felt like a theme park. The show was plodding and methodical though it did not lack for interest, with 50 Cent and crew mugging and throwing down rhymes against the heavy beats coming over the speakers. There was an obvious lack of any real communication between 50 Cent and the audience since few could have had any idea what he was saying, even when he spoke directly to them in his thick drawl. The only time he really tried to hype the crowd was toward the end of the show when he prodded them directly in call and response cant, "Say, G-Unit, G-Unit, G-Unit" and a moment later, "Say Slim Shady, Slim Shady, Slim Shady," actually getting a tepid smattering of a response. Many of them may have recognized the brand names he yelled in their direction—they may even have been wearing them—but it is inconceivable that many of them could actually have guessed what he had been rapping about all night. The kind of inner-city desolation, gang violence, and street-level drug hustling that produced 50 Cent was half a world away and almost unimaginable in post-communist Prague even after nearly twenty years since the fall of the Berlin Wall.

For many of the kids in the audience that night, this was undoubtedly the closest they had ever come to African Americans and perhaps the first time many of them had seen a black male outside the mediated confines of television, film, and video games. In the absence of any real and shared understanding through language or culture, the vicarious gangsterism that 50 Cent made available to them as entertainment suggests how important the visual commodity has become in the context of popular music since the 1980s. What was on display at the show was not simply a concert of beats and rhymes, but a representation of racial difference as deviance, informed by an alluring sense of the forbidden in a culture used to conformity—the swagger of a real American outlaw, a black gangsta from the street who had taken nine shots and lived to rap about it. The spectacularized, larger than life image of 50 Cent, drenched in spotlights, gold chains, and diamond earrings, worked as much at the level of myth as the level of entertainment—50 Cent represented the myth of the bad nigger in living color, a talisman whose power could be vicariously accessed for the price of a ticket. It was not wholly unlike watching the spectacle of powerful lions paraded before an audience that is fully aware of the danger the beasts pose but comforted in knowing that it is a performance, that the powerful animals are tightly controlled and leashed. One is safe to gaze from afar at that which is both frightening and fascinating.

The apprehension that I often invited strolling through the heterogeneous streets of Prague was not lost on me. At least once my presence on the street was met with recoil that verged on terror by an adolescent boy who could very well have been at the 50 Cent show, when I approached him to ask for directions. He feared me as if I had stepped out of a violent gangster-themed video game—my Frantz Fanon moment. It would be simple enough to pass off such a reaction as racism, but that would be too simple, and I do not believe, quite accurate. For many whites, like the white youth at the 50 Cent show, the black male body that functions primarily at the level of myth can only be apprehended at a distance, close enough to be consumed but far enough away so as not to threaten. In the post-MTV world of video culture and the post-hardcore rap world of commodity thugs, mediated images of the black male body remain a fantasy of masculine desire that encapsulates extreme alternatives of heroism and villainy for white and other youth who often have few other references for black American culture.

Performatives of blackness, hybridity, cultural borrowing, fetishization of the black body, and strategies of appropriation by nonblack actors that suggest a love of black cultural expressions arguably intersect at dangerous crossroads when they reify and exploit objectified and pejorative representations of a racial Other reduced to consumer commodity in cultural projects that do not advance progressive or anti-racist agendas. The popularity of blackface minstrelsy from the early 1800s to the Civil War and afterward did not generate popular white support for Reconstruction in the American South; the cultural revolution generated by 1950s rhythm and blues, Elvis Presley, and rock 'n' roll did not translate into widespread white support for *Brown v. Board of Education* and the desegregation of Southern society; America's fascination with Motown, Stax, and 1960s soul music did not assuage a backlash to Dr. Martin Luther King Jr.'s civil rights movement in southern states to eliminate Jim Crow laws and guarantee black citizens the right to vote. Conjectures, therefore, about hip-hop's contribution to fostering a more benevolent cultural hybridity and cross-racial tolerance may still be premature.

Richard Thompson Ford is quite correct in his observation that racial minorities, especially those in the so-called underclass most likely to display racially distinctive affectations and behavior in speech, manner, and dress, are socially demonized because society has abandoned any serious effort to integrate them into the American mainstream. On the other hand, the popularization of hardcore styles of hip-hop and urban street affectations that have become synonymous with black urban culture have not simply normalized ghetto culture, but transfigured it as racialized commodity and (re)inserted it into the popular mainstream culture, so that many young black urban males may have few incentives to try and conform to mainstream expectations of appearance and speech or pursue meaningful life goals beyond the street. For white and other young males who engage hip-hop culture, and this is increasingly true outside the United States, the representational practices that have dominated hip-hop music since the late 1980s have produced a generation for whom the black gangsta and thug have become the most compelling representations of masculinity available to them. One of the most problematic aspects of such adulation is certainly that it breeds a kind of racial spectatorship in which black masculinity is objectified as spectacle, perpetuating myths about the black male as brute.

The subtext of a maligned and aggrieved black subjectivity both informs and troubles the perception of masculinity within the context of hardcore rap music and culture. The essentially performative nature of the representations contained within them are often taken more literally than figuratively even by otherwise well-meaning and reasonable people. Perhaps this is the case because these representations are performed in the register of the real in a way that has not previously been observed in popular music performance or has been made so widely available through the apparatus of the culture industry. The deeper implications and challenges for youth who appropriate, admire, consume, and transform African American cultural expressions is to move beyond such fetishizing representations of blackness and masculinities to embrace the transformational possibilities of racial transgression. The performances of the urban gangsta and thug by African American male actors and the consumption of these images by non-African American male actors more often than not contribute little to progressive politics and anti-racist agendas. While it is on the one hand difficult to criticize young African American inner-city males with few life options for prospering through marketing gangsta and thug street fantasies, most white youth, on the other hand, are encouraged and empowered to engage a field of racial play for which there are few real consequences and nothing at stake.

The production of faux black subjectivity and the performance of racial difference by white actors for whom socio-cultural hegemony sustains political and economic agendas and advantages should no longer be taken for granted, nor should they go unexamined. Whiteness as a socially constructed ground of being that masks itself through the performance of the Other has escaped substantial critique in contemporary popular music in the last quarter century except by a handful of scholars. African American hardcore rappers, however, also attempt to obscure the same historical power relationships in order to (re)interject themselves into a different and ahistorical moment, not as the *niggers* swinging from trees in the South with ropes around their necks, but the *niggas* swigging from bottles of Armand de Brignac in penthouses with gold chains around their necks. On the other hand, perhaps it is better to posture as the angry black man, as the drug dealer, pimp, hustler, or gangbanger and get paid for it than to continue to live the life. I do not begrudge Snoop Dogg, the Game, 50 Cent, Jay-Z, or others the right to earn fabulous sums of money when they would probably have few life choices beyond what they are now being paid very handsomely to do. Nonetheless, one must wonder whether such representations do not carry a cultural price in the long run, what I have referred to as a "Bert Williams problem" in fact, since the performance of masculinity by hardcore hip-hop artists is both a reaction to racist stereotypes and a (re)assertion of them that allows and encourages their emulation by others for financial gain. As cultural critics, we should be interested in how the ubiquitousness of these representations continues to transform the public and popular sphere and what it means that youth in other parts of the globe who consume hip-hop music do not distinguish between hip-hop culture and African American culture, or between imagined black demons and real black people.

If nineteenth-century minstrelsy offered a national stage for enacting the fears and anxieties of those caught up in the traumatic transitioning from a largely rural and agrarian nation to urban industrialization, hip-hop has similarly offered a global stage for the postindustrial alienation and discontent of adolescent youth at the end of the twentieth century confronted with fewer blue-collar opportunities in some ways but in others entering a new and startling age of new hi-tech, digital possibilities. Yet we need to continue to try and understand the complexity of social and cultural meanings behind what it is that is being performed, by whom, for whom, and to what effect. It is not insignificant to recall that it was not uncommon for minstrel troupes to perform in towns where whites had never seen a real black person and so took their imaginings of African Americans from the reductive caricatures of what Mark Twain called the *Real Nigger Show*. The towering legacy of someone as important as Bert Williams, who also had the right to make a living and who made a very good one performing in greasepaint, nonetheless played to white racial prejudice and helped to sustain the legacy of Jim Crow in the Deep South. The legacy of both black and white minstrel performers instantiated deeply ingrained pejorative representations of blacks into popular culture that troubled discourses around race, public policy, and black social advancement for the next century. Whether this will be the case with rap performance remains unclear at this point, even more than a quarter century out. We can only to look to the past and assess the present, warily, and with hope.

Perhaps the most interesting footnote to all of this is that in 2008, the United States elected for the first time a presidential candidate with a known African heritage—Barack Obama is in fact more African American than most of those in the United States who claim the label since he only has to look back one generation to a father who *actually was* born in Africa. Earlier I called him the first hip-hop president since his election probably would not have happened without the engagement in the political process by legions of fans who participate in the music culture of hip-hop and for whom Obama represented not just an end to politics as usual, but to a status quo that only legitimated American power expressed through whiteness. Just as important, Obama had credibility with, and the financial support of, major figures associated with the culture, none more significant than Jay-Z, whose music the presidential candidate famously carried around on his iPod. Millions of dollars that financed Obama's campaign were mobilized through this community and his very real connection to it. This historical moment finally realized what some had worked toward for decades, the socio-political harnessing of the hip-hop nation in a way that could be turned into something real, tangible, and that mattered at the highest levels of our society, like putting a person of color in the White House.

Obama's transformation of American politics lies certainly in the fact that he broke down perhaps the most impenetrable racial glass ceiling in the United States, one that many assumed would not be broken in our lifetime. Beyond what his obvious intelligence, political skills, and ambitions for the United States allows him to accomplish, certainly what is also obvious is that he challenges hundreds of years of historically pejorative representations of black males and the strategies enacted to contain them. He represents a compelling alternative model of black masculinity that merely affirms that such men have certainly always existed in American society. Obama offers a critical anti-hegemonic counterpoint to the meta-narrative of black males in the United States and to popular culture fascination with the bad nigger, reasserting the role of the African American male as bad man in the folkloric sense of the term in that he works courageously for not simply what is best for himself and his associates, but what is best for his community, which in his case encompasses the entire nation, as it must and as it should. In a country that has historically sought to delegitimize African American bad man figures who have represented threats to the racial status quo and to institutions of American power and authority, and who have tried to usher in values of social justice and inclusion for marginalized communities, Obama's moment is nothing less than a promise that more such moments can now be dreamed and realized, and by people who may have heretofore believed them unachievable.

It is important to also note, however, that as much as many think of Obama as the first black or African American president, framing him solely in those terms is reductive on a number of levels, not the least of which is that he is biracial, the product of a union between a black man and a white woman. It is only our unquestioned and perhaps unwitting allegiance to the so-called one-drop doctrine of presumed racial inferiority and superiority between black and white that allows the perpetuation of this particular myth and the denial of half of Obama's family heritage. More important, perhaps, it argues against the other compelling thing Obama represents, the triumph of progressive, antiracist social politics, something that politicians in the Deep South have effectively prevented for years through socio-political race-baiting. The false idea that white skin conveyed a social status enforced by illegitimate laws has primarily benefited a privileged elite and prevented deeper discussions about issues of class and gender inequality that disfranchised poor whites as much as poor blacks. Obama's victory is not the triumph of a post-racist society, but it may be the promise of one, embodied both in his person and in the fact that the hip-hop nation is more diverse and pluralistic than many would imagine only consuming much of what is made available through the popular culture industry. Obama's moment is also hip-hop's moment to move beyond the racial stereotypes that continue to define it in the global marketplace of commerce. The question of whether or not it will is a serious one. It is one thing to speak truth to power, but it may be another thing altogether to speak truth to money.

# Appendix

Robert Plant Armstrong's Distribution of Affecting Media among Forms

| | Sculpture | Dance | Graphic | Music | Architecture | Drama | Narrative | Costume | Poetry |
|---|---|---|---|---|---|---|---|---|---|
| Situation | X | X | X | X | | X | X | | X |
| Surface | X | X | X | | X | | | X | |
| Color | X | | X | | X | | | X | |
| Volume | X | X | | | X | | | | |
| Tone | | | | X | | | | | * |
| Movement | X | X | | | | X | | X | |
| Word | | | | | | X | X | | X |
| Relationality | X | X | X | X | X | X | X | X | X |
| Experience | X | X | X | X | X | X | X | X | X |

*I have omitted tone while recognizing that it exists in tonal language as an element—but of meaning, not of poetry. [author's note]

# Notes

## Introduction

1. Morrison, 8.

2. While we can hardly speak anymore of a single African American culture, I am addressing African American culture in and of the United States, although this as well is no longer reducible to a single homogeneous group of socio-culturally and politically monolithic black people, if the essentialism debates have taught us anything. I will attempt to be as specific as possible here about whom it is I am discussing. I would argue, however, that particularly in American society, racial identities as they are lived through the daily social, cultural, and political interactions among members of different communities are not as nuanced as academicians would have it. A discussion of racial identities and the lived experience of race does not disregard the essentialist argument, but acknowledges its limitations.

3. Menand, 149.

4. Menand, 155.

5. Several notable books from this period include Joseph Boskin's *Sambo* (1986), John Roberts' *From Trickster to Bad Man* (1989), Richard Majors and Janet Mancini Billson's *Cool Pose* (1992), Tricia Rose's *Black Noise* (1994), bell hooks' *Outlaw Culture* (1994), Eric Lott's *Love and Theft* (1995), Susan Gubar's *Racechanges* (1997), W. T. Lhamon's *Raising Cain* (1998), Michael Bertrand's *Race, Rock and Elvis* (2000), Greg Dimitriadis' *Performing Identity/Performing Culture* (2001), Cheryl Keyes' *Rap Music and Street Consciousness* (2002), Murray Forman's *The Hood Comes First* (2002), Leon Wynter's *American Skin* (2002), Stephen Whitehead's *Men and Masculinities* (2002), E. Patrick Johnson's *Appropriating Blackness* (2003), Eithne Quinn's *Nuthin' But A "g" Thang* (2005), and Linda Tucker's *Lockstep and Dance* (2007), among many others.

6. Morrison, 6.

7. Radano and Bohlman, 5.

8. Radano and Bohlman, 5.

9. T. Rose, 227.

## Chapter 1: Shadow and Act

1. Jafa, 246.

2. The character of Jim Crow prior to the Civil War was often used to justify the system of plantation slavery since it put forth the image of a simple-minded people happy with their lot and incapable of surviving in freedom. The socially inept Zip Coon, on the other hand, fanned fears of the intrusion of black bodies into white space by posing the impossibility of black adaptation and integration into polite northern society. In practice, the performances of these characters were often more complex and often subversive. However, in the representational language of affect and imagery, they had a largely deleterious effect in shaping the racial imagination where blacks were concerned because their embedded socio-political messages were traded as seemingly innocuous cultural artifacts of pleasure.

3. Hall, 239.

4. L. Tucker, 159.

5. Ellison, 48.

6. Lhamon, 44.

7. Lott, 6.

8. Burnim and Maultsby, 189.

9. Burnim and Maultsby, 189.

10. Harris, 9.

11. Harris, 40.

12. Gray, 36.

13. Morrison, 52.

14. Jafa, 247.

15. hooks, 23.

16. Crunden, 202.

17. Crunden, 173.

18. Crunden, 6.

19. Delgado and Stefancic, 170–71.

20. Davis also lamented the absence of dignified images of black women on jazz album covers and used images of his wife Frances Davis on the covers of his albums *In Person Friday and Saturday Nights at the Blackhawk* (1961), *Someday My Prince Will Come*, (1961) and *E.S.P.* (1965). His second wife, Betty Davis, adorned the cover for *Filles de Kilimanjaro* (1969) and future wife, Cicely Tyson, was chosen for the cover of *Sorcerer* (1967).

## Chapter 2: The Fire This Time

1. Root, 73.

2. Root, 73.

3. Root, 73.

4. Root, 79.

5. hooks (1992), 23.

6. For a fuller discussion of the critical role of b-boying in hip-hop culture, see Joe Schloss' *Foundation: B-Boys, B-Girls, and Hip-hop Culture in New York* (New York: Oxford University Press, 2009).

7. Kaplan, 12.

8. Ruby, 65.

9. Fraser and Greco, 1.

10. Lott, 117.

11. Kiesling, 281.

12. Binnie, 123.

13. Fanon, 26.

14. Hall (1996).

15. Lott, 92.

16. McDonald, 283.

17. Bordo, 37.

18. C. Johnson, 610.

19. Frederickson and Roberts, 175.

20. Frederickson and Roberts, 175.

21. Frederickson and Roberts, 175.

22. The line that demarcates new school rap from old school rap is quite permeable, since old school styles were still performed well into the new school era. Some simple demarcation points, nonetheless, mark the beginning of these periods—old school in 1979 with the release of "Rapper's Delight," new school in 1983 with Run-DMC's releases "Sucker MCs" and "It's Like That." Hardcore rap as a genre may be marked from 1988 with the appearance of N.W.A. and the album *Straight Outta Compton*, notwithstanding influential earlier work by Schoolly D, Boogie Down Productions, and Ice-T. The contemporary era of radio-friendly hardcore styles begin with Dr. Dre's *The Chronic* in 1992.

23. Norfleet, 362.

24. Frith, 219.

25. Frith, 209.

26. Lawrence Grossberg in Wilson-Brown and McCarthy, 355.

27. Gilroy (1993), 270.

28. E. P. Johnson, 7.

29. Stallybrass and White, 104.

30. Hannerz, 313.

31. Frazier's work actually spanned categories of class, and includes *The Negro Family in the United States* (1939), *Negro Youth at the Crossways* (1940), and *Black Bourgeoisie* (1957).

32. Hannerz, 315.

33. Hannerz, 313–14.

34. The National Advisory Commission on Civil Disorder, chaired by Illinois Governor Otto Kerner, was tasked by President Lyndon Johnson with determining the causes of a series of riots by blacks in major urban cities across the United States in 1967. The commission issued its report in 1968, detailing in part, a nation "moving toward two societies, one black, one white, separate and unequal."

35. Mailer. No page numbering.

36. Mailer.

37. Awkward, 180

38. Samuels, 251.

39. Samuels, 251.

40. Wong, 78.

## Chapter 3: Affective Gestures

1. The term *fresh* in hip-hop is not far from its normative meaning, suggesting something that is new, original, and wholly unique in some way so as to mark it from that which has come before it, even if it borrows from and transforms that which has come before it, which is often the case.

2. Barthes, 62.

3. Stock, 90.

4. Stock, 91.

5. Forman, 16.

6. Pollock, 9.

7. Schechner, 326.

8. Goffman, 91.

9. Armstrong (1971); Robert Plant, *The Affecting Presence: An Essay in Humanistic Anthropology* (Urbana: University of Illinois Pres, 1971).

10. See the appendix for Armstrong's original table.

11. Armstrong (1975); Robert Plant, *Wellspring: On the Myth and Source of Culture* (Berkeley: University of California Press, 1975).

12. Armstrong (1975), xii.

13. Armstrong (1975), 49.

14. Keyes (2004), 32–33.

15. Keyes, 34.

16. In "The Photograph Turntable and Performance Practice in Hip Hop Music" (1996), an ethnographic inquiry into the performance practices of turntablism, I isolated the foundational technical skills, physical dexterity, and musicality required by a competent turntable performer. That investigation was my education into hip-hop culture, and it led me also to thinking about issues beyond those purely music-related, including race, masculinity, and performance. The subject of that ethnographic inquiry, a Seattle area DJ who went by the name B-Mello, was a young white male who for some time impressed me as being a very light-skinned African American, so much had he adopted the performance codes and mannerisms of young black urban males. I found his metamorphosis intriguing. It would be the genesis for the present book.

17. These are generally accepted as the four traditional pillars of hip-hop, but there is a case to be made that beatboxing, the rhythmic vocables used as accompaniment to rhymes in the early days of hip-hop and that developed its own artistry and a list of legendary performers, deserves to be counted as a fifth pillar

18. By *place* I mean the importance of specific geographical locations such as the Bronx, Queens, and Compton. By space I mean the way in which people in the culture such as graffiti artists and muralists would often appropriate the use of mainly public property, including trains, buildings, and other available surfaces to create underground art. In the early days of hip-hop in New York City, b-boys would often put down slabs of cardboard on public sidewalks to break for tips, another kind of appropriation of public space. Even

the use of giant boom boxes blaring hip-hop, ubiquitous in the late 1970s and early 1980s, may be seen as a transgressive invasion of public space.

19. I am using Christopher Small's term *musicking* in conjunction with Goffman's idea of the performance of the everyday to embrace both professional or *performing artists* and social or *performing actors* who participate in the culture. In this sense, then, these allow for the embracing of a broad array of extra-musical elements that may be seen as performative, including but not limited to the corporeal body, public space, commodity items, the use of color, context, personal experience, urban vernacular language, and words themselves.

20. Gray, 149.

21. Gray, 148.

22. Gray, 151.

23. Gray, 147.

24. Gray, 36.

25. This idea does not mean to suggest that such geographical areas are racially isolated and exclusive any more than music culture areas can be discussed as hermetically sealed. I merely suggest that those spaces that have produced the primary articulations of hip-hop aesthetics and practices have tended to be cultural spheres where black people live and interact daily, but which have certainly in many instances been socio-economically marginalized.

26. Forman, 84.

27. In the 1980s, hip-hop songs such as "The Message" and "P.S.K. What Does it Mean" made the inner city the focus of hard-edged ghetto narratives, while "The Bridge is Over" and "South Bronx" were critical in establishing the importance of specific geographic locations. With *Straight Outta Compton* in 1988, specific geographic places and the importance of articulating them would become tied to both individual identity and group affiliation.

28. Foucault, 195–228.

29. H. Rose, 5.

30. Lewis, 83.

31. Kelley, 191.

32. Whitehead, 185.

33. Whitehead, 195.

34. Butler, 174.

35. Butler, 175.

36. The so-called b-boy stance—arms folded across the chest and head slightly tilted to the side—may be the most iconic body posture in hip-hop.

37. Majors and Billson, 73.

38. See Maultsby's discussion of the soul music aesthetic in *African American Music: An Introduction*, ed. Mellonee Burnim and Portia Maultsby (New York: Routledge, 2006), 279.

39. Stallybrass and White, 135.

40. This refers to the folk notion of black signifying practices in which the signifier may carp, cajole, needle, and generally make fun of another person surreptitiously or behind her or his back; it can "denote speaking with the hands and eyes" and involve parody

and misdirection as exemplified in the character of the "Signifying Monkey" in the epic "toast" of the same name. See Mitchell-Kernan's "Signifying, Loud-Talking and Marking," in *Signifyin(g), Sanctifying' & Slam Dunking. A Reader in African American Expressive Culture*, ed. Gena Dagel Caponi (Amherst: University of Massachusetts Press, 1999).

41. hooks (1995b), 131.

42. hooks (1995b), 131.

43. This term is by now largely considered old school and rarely used, but I use it here as a catch-all term to suggest not only clothing but all manner of adornment and accessories that play upon the surface of the body and thus may be considered part of the presentation or performance of self.

44. Wynter, 3.

45. Samuels, 244.

46. The introduction of the bandana into Southern California West Coast gang culture in particular likely comes from Mexican American *cholo* culture, which contributed a number of other significant items to West Coast rap culture, including an affinity for plaid shirts and lowrider automobiles.

47. T. Rose (1994), 25.

48. Wilson, 159.

49. Langer, 211.

50. Langer, 222.

51. Typically, a needle indicator tipping into the excessive high end of a volume meter set off with a red area and warning of possible sound distortion. See the discussion in T. Rose (1994), 74.

52. T. Rose (1994), 63.

53. Carter, 203.

54. For a more sustained critical discussion of rap's poetics and verbal style, see Adam Bradley's *Book of Rhymes: The Poetics of Hip Hop* (New York. Basic Civitas, 2009).

55. Shanahan (2008), 7.

56. I make a number of references throughout this book to the black underclass. I think there are stark differences between what we have long understood as the working class and the more recent phenomenon of the underclass that have to do certainly with class but that must also be viewed in terms of the retrenchment in the War on Poverty, the dismantling of the welfare state, the persistence of racism, and the failure of public education, among other factors. For a fuller understanding of the social dimensions of the underclass, see William Julius Wilson, ed., *The Ghetto Underclass: Social Science Perspectives* (Newbury Park: Sage Publications, 1993) and William Julius William, *The Truly Disadvantaged: The Inner City, the Underclass, and Public Policy* (Chicago: University of Chicago Press, 1990).

57. See Keyes' discussion of provocative words and their evocative power in *Rap Music and Street Consciousness*.

58. See Roger Abrahams' *Deep Down in the Jungle: Negro Narrative Folklore from the Streets of Philadelphia* (1954); Bruce Jackson's *Get Your Ass in the Water and Swim Like Me* (1974); and *The Life, The Lore and Folk Poetry of the Black Hustler* by Dennis Wepman et al. (1976).

59. Gates.

60. An illustrative example was the attention the Southern California hardcore rap group N.W.A. received from law enforcement authorities, including a letter an assistant director of the FBI sent to the group's recording company, after the release of their satirical 1988 single "Fuck Tha Police," which verbally depicted the killing of police officers in Los Angeles in response to abusive policing practices by the Los Angeles Police Department. Four years earlier, however, Arnold Schwarzenegger's 1984 dramatic film *The Terminator* depicted in graphic imagery the violent slaughter of an entire police precinct without much note of concern. No one reasonably expected attacks on police departments because of the film, but many were willing to suspend rational judgment in the case of N.W.A. and young black males from Watts and South Central.

61. T. Rose (1994), 125.

62. I discuss the intrusion of crack cocaine into the culture of hip-hop more fully in the following chapter.

63. Ford, 298.

64. Ford, 298.

65. Ford, 301.

66. Ford, 302.

## Chapter 4: Real Niggas

1. Roberts, 177.

2. Roberts, 6.

3. Gilmore, 102.

4. In 2009, the U.S. Congress approved a resolution, first introduced in 2004, urging President Barack Obama to grant a posthumous pardon to Johnson for his 1913 conviction under the Mann Act, also known as the White Slave Traffic Act. Senator John McCain of Arizona was the lead sponsor of the Senate resolution, which states in part that the pardon would "expunge a racially motivated abuse of the prosecutorial authority of the Federal Government from the annals of criminal justice in the United States." As of this writing, President Obama has not granted the pardon.

5. Jefferson, 92.

6. Jefferson, 84.

7. Jefferson, 94.

8. Jefferson, 94.

9. Lott, 118.

10. Roberts, 215.

11. Messerschmidt, 6.

12. Messerschmidt, 6.

13. Messerschmidt, 6.

14. Messerschmidt, 43.

15. Messerschmidt, 46.

16. Monson, 419.

17. L. Tucker, 18.

18. Lively, 226.

19. Lively, 232.

20. Lively, 241.

21. Lively, 237.

22. Lively, 238.

23. Samuels, 242.

24. The convictions of Poindexter and North were overturned on appeal. Weinberger and others were later pardoned during the administration of President George H. W. Bush.

25. On April 17, 1986, the Associated Press published a news article entitled "U.S. Concedes Contras Linked to Drugs, But Denies Leadership Involved."

26. On July 23, 1998, Justice Department Inspector General Michael Bromwich issued a report showing Reagan administration officials were aware of cocaine traffickers in the Contra operation. A report issued on October 8, 1998, by the CIA inspector general gave evidence that money from drug trafficking was used by Oliver North at the National Security Administration for Contra operations. Gary Webb was found dead in 2004 from two gunshot wounds to the head. His death was officially ruled a suicide. (Source: The National Security Archive, The Gelman Library, George Washington University, Washington, D.C.)

27. See Nick Schou's 2006 book *Kill the Messenger: How the CIA's Crack Cocaine Controversy Destroyed Journalist Gary Webb* (New York: National Books, 2006).

28. Levitt and Dubner, 100.

29. Levitt and Dubner, 103.

30. Levitt and Dubner, 103.

31. Levitt and Dubner, 212.

32. Levitt and Dubner, 122.

33. Levitt and Dubner, 122.

34. As of this writing (December 4, 2010, which happens to be Jay-Z's forty-first birthday), the book had risen to the third position on *The New York Times* list of bestselling hardcover nonfiction works.

35. Carter, 10.

36. Carter, 18–19.

37. Carter, 71.

38. Carter, 12.

39. Clockers, and clocking, refer to street-level crack dealing by organized teams who put in long hours distributing "work" (drugs) to customers. An eightball is an eighth of an ounce of cocaine.

40. Carter, 12–13.

41. Carter, 12.

42. Carter, 17.

43. Carter, 17.

44. Carter, 26.

45. Forbes 400. *The Richest People in America*. 2010 Edition. Special issue.

46. Carter, 158.

47. Carter, 130.

48. Carter, 265.

49. Chang, 137.

50. Lipsitz, 5.
51. Lipsitz, 4.
52. Lipsitz, 5.


## Chapter 5: Race Rebels

1. Monson, 397.
2. Monson, 398.
3. Monson, 398.
4. Monson, 404.
5. According to a February 11, 1946, article in *Downbeat* magazine ("Dizzy Gillespie's Style, Its Meaning Analyzed") performers also imitated Gillespie's standing posture while performing, which resembled the figure "S," which he apparently affected because he was too apathetic to stand erectly. This stance would later become iconic with Miles Davis and currently with many performers in rap music.
6. Monson, 402.
7. Monson, 419.
8. Sweeney, 254.
9. Finson, 162.
10. Boskin, 81.
11. Garofalo, 125.
12. Szatmary, 24.
13. Grossberg (1997), 71.
14. Grossberg (1997), 71.
15. Lipsitz, 54.
16. Lipsitz, 54.
17. Rux, 37.
18. Lipsitz, 55.
19. Lipsitz, 62.
20. Lipsitz, 66.
21. Keyes, 90.
22. The involvement of Latinos in hip-hop has been underrepresented in much of the popular and academic literature. Nonetheless, it is a vibrant underground scene and has a rich history of performers. This history is discussed in the DVD *Pass The Mic!* (Safada Y Sano Productions, 2002), directed by Richard Montes.
23. Bernard, 54.
24. Bernard, 54.
25. McDonald, 281.
26. The nylon cap he is referring to is the doo-rag, a stylized version of a woman's nylon pantyhose cut short and worn by black men to protect "processed" or chemically treated hair. It is also linked to social deviance and criminality since nylon stockings pulled down over the face become cheap disguises for use in committing crimes. The cap has become a fashion accessory for young men in urban gang culture but has been appropriated as casual street attire in the hip-hop community. Rappers such as Snoop Dogg, Jay-Z, Eminem, and 50 Cent have worn them in public and in photographs.

27. Seabrook, 3.

28. Seabrook, 4.

29. Wynter, 37.

30. Dimitriadis, 24.

31. West, 121.

32. Hall (2003), 265.

33. Roediger, 654.

34. Anderson, 14.

35. Rux, 25.

36. Horrorcore is a subgenre of hardcore hip-hop that indulges macabre themes such as homicide, rape, and torture taken from horror and slasher films but that also borrow from heavy metal rock and bands such as Black Sabbath and Judas Priest whose material often includes dark themes around death and the occult.

37. Rux, 28.

38. Roediger, 661.

39. Ford, 335.

40. Ford, 25.

41. Ford, 337.

42. Personal communication with Brother Ali via telephone interview on September 2, 2003.

43. The Stop the Violence Movement was a coalition of hip-hop artists united against violence in the black community that was organized by KRS-ONE shortly after the murder of his Boogie Down Productions partner Scott La Rock. In 1989, the coalition released the 12-inch single "Self Destruction," donating the proceeds to the National Urban League.

44. Newitz and Wray, 3.

45. hooks (1990), 22.

46. hooks (1990), 20.

47. Newitz and Wray, 5.

48. Newitz and Wray, 4.

49. Dr. West used this term in a 2004 public lecture given in Seattle, Washington, in discussing the 2001 attack on the World Trade Center and subsequent feelings expressed to him by whites of being abused and hated, which he compared to the Otherization of African Americans in the United States.

50. hooks (1990), 20.

51. hooks (1990) 21.

52. hooks (1990) 21.

53. hooks (1990) 21.

# References

Abrahams, Roger D. *Deep Down in the Jungle: Negro Narrative Folklore from the Streets of Philadelphia*. Piscataway: Aldine Transaction.

Anderson, Benedict. *Imagined Communities*. London: Verso, 1992.

Anderson, Victor. *Beyond Ontological Blackness. An Essay on African American Religious and Cultural Criticism*. New York: Continuum, 1995.

Armstrong, Robert Plant. *The Affecting Presence. An Essay in Humanistic Anthropology*. Urbana: University of Illinois Press, 1971.

———. *Wellspring: On the Myth and Source of Culture*. Berkeley. University of California Press, 1975.

Awkward, Michael, *Negotiating Difference. Race, Gender and the Politics of Positionality*. Chicago: University of Chicago Press, 1995.

Barth, Frederik. *Ethnic Groups and Boundaries: The Social Organization of Cultural Difference*. London: George Allen & Unwin, 1969. Pp. 9–38.

Barthes, Roland. *Image, Music, Text: Selected Essays*. New York: Hill and Wang, 1977.

Bernard, James. "Why the World Is After Vanilla Ice." *The New York Times*, February 3, 1991.

Binnie, Jon. *The Globalization of Sexuality*. London: Sage, 2004.

Blauner, Robert. "Black Culture: Myth or Reality?" In *African American Anthropology*, edited by Norman Whitten. New York: The Free Press, 1970.

Bordo, Susan. "Reading the Male Body." *Michigan Quarterly Review* (1993): 696.

Boskin, Joseph. *Sambo. The Rise & Demise of an American Jester*. New York: Oxford University Press, 1986.

Burnim, Mellonee and Maultsby, Portia. *African American Music: An Introduction*. New York: Routledge, 2006.

Butler, Judith. *Gender Trouble. Feminism and the Subversion of Identity*. London: Routledge, 1990.

Caponi, Gena Dagel, ed. *Signifyin(g), Sanctifying' & Slam Dunking. A Reader in African American Expressive Culture*. Amherst: University of Massachusetts Press, 1999.

Carter, Shawn. *Jay-Z Decoded*. New York. Spiegel & Grau, 2010.

Chang, Jeff. *Can't Stop, Won't Stop: A History of the Hip-hop Generation*. New York: St. Martin's Press, 2005.

Cheney, Charise L. "Phallic/ies and His(s)tories: Masculinity and the Black Nationalist Tradition, From Slave Spirituals to Rap Music." Doctoral dissertation, University of Illinois, Urbana-Champaign, 1999.

Cohen, Anthony. *The Symbolic Construction of Community*. Chichester: Ellis Horwood Ltd., 1985.

Cohen, Sara. "Men Making A Scene. Rock Music and the Production of Gender." In *Sexing the Groove. Popular Music and Gender*, edited by S. Whiteley. London: Routledge, 1997.

Cornyetz, Nina. "Fetishized Blackness: Hip-hop and Racial Desire in Contemporary Japan." *Social Text* 41(Winter 1994): 113–39.

Crunden, Robert M. *Body and Soul. The Making of American Modernism*. New York: Basic Books, 2000.

Delgado, Richard, and Jean Stefancic. "Images of the Outsider in American Law and Culture." In *Critical White Studies: Looking Behind the Mirror*, edited by R. Delgado. Philadelphia: Temple University Press, 1997.

Denzin, Norman K. *Reading Race: Hollywood and the Cinema of Racial Violence*. London: Sage, 2002.

Dimitriadis, Greg. *Performing Identity/Performing Culture. Hip-hop as Text, Pedagogy and Lived Practice*. New York: Peter Lang, 2001.

Dubrowa, Corey. "Throne of Blood. Rap Supernova 50 Cent Is the Latest King of the Hip-hop Nation." *Seattle Weekly* (2004): 45.

Dyson, Michael Eric. *Holler If You Hear Me: Searching for Tupac Shakur*. New York: Basic Civitas Books, 2001.

Ellison, Ralph. "Change the Joke and Slip the Yoke." In *Shadow and Act*. New York: Random House, 1972 [1958].

Fanon, Frantz. *Black Skin, White Masks*. Trans. Charles Lam Markmann. London: MacGibbon & Kee, 1968. .

Finson, J. W. *The Voices That Are Gone*. Oxford: Oxford University Press, 1994.

Ford, Richard Thompson. *The Race Card. How Bluffing About Bias Makes Race Relations Worse*. New York: Farrar, Straus and Giroux, 2008.

Forman, Murray. *The Hood Comes First: Race, Space and Place in Rap and Hip-Hop*. Middletown: Wesleyan University Press, 2002.

Foucault, Michel. *Discipline & Punish: The Birth of the Prison*. New York: Vintage Books, 1995

Fraser, Mariam, and Monica Greco. *The Body: A Reader*. New York: Routledge, 2005.

Fredrickson, Barbara, and Tomi-Ann Roberts. "Objectification Theory: Toward Understanding Women's Lived Experiences and Mental Health Risks." *Psychology of Women Quarterly* 21, no. 2 (1997): 173–206.

Frith, Simon. *Performing Rites. On The Value of Popular Music*. Cambridge, Mass.: Harvard University Press, 1996.

Frith, Simon, and Andrew Goodwin. *On Record: Rock, Pop and the Written Word*. New York: Routledge. 1990.

Garofalo, Reebee. *Rocking Out. Popular Music in the USA*. Upper Saddle River: Prentice Hall, 2002 [1997].

Gates, Henry Louis. "Live Crew, Decoded." *The New York Times*. June 19, 1990, A23.

Geertz, Clifford. *The Interpretation of Culture*. New York: Basic Books, 1973.

Gilmore, Al-Tony. *Bad Nigger! The National Impact of Jack Johnson*. Port Washington: National University Publications, 1975.

Gilroy, Paul. *The Black Atlantic. Modernity and Double Consciousness*. Cambridge, Mass.: Harvard University Press, 1993.

———. *Against Race. Imagining Political Culture Beyond the Color Line*. Cambridge, Mass.: Harvard University Press, 2000.

Goffman, Erving. *The Presentation of Self in Everyday Life*. Garden City: Doubleday Anchor, 1959.

Gray, Herman. *Watching Race: Television and the Struggle for Blackness*. Minneapolis: University of Minnesota Press, 1995.

Grossberg, Lawrence. "History, Politics and Postmodernism: Stuart Hall and Cultural Studies." In *Stuart Hall: Critical Dialogues in Cultural Studies*, edited by D.a.K.-H.C. Morley. New York: Routledge, 1996.

———. *Dancing In Spite of Myself: Essays on Popular Culture*. Durham: Duke University Press, 1997.

Gubar, Susan. *Racechanges: White Skin, Black Face in American Culture*. New York: Oxford University Press, 1997.

Halberstam, Judith. *Female Masculinity*. Durham: Duke University Press, 1998.

Hall, Stuart. *Race: The Floating Signifier*. Northampton: Media Education Foundation, 1996.

———. *Representation: Cultural Representations and Signifying Practices*. Ed. S. Hall. London: Sage, 2003.

Hannerz, Ulf. "What Ghetto Males Are Like: Another Look." In *Afro-American Anthropology: Contemporary Perspectives*, edited by N.a.J.F.S. Whitten. New York: The Free Press, 1970.

Harris, Michael D. *Colored Pictures. Race and Visual Representation*. Chapel Hill: University of North Carolina Press, 2003.

Hartmann, Douglas, and Roderick Ferguson. "Introduction: Rethinking Race." In *Rethinking Race, Troubling Empiricism*. University of California, San Diego Critical Monograph Series.

hooks, bell. *Yearning: Race, Gender, and Cultural Politics*. Boston: South End Press. 1990.

———. *Black Looks. Race and Representation*. Boston: South End Press, 1992.

———. *Outlaw Culture: Resisting Representations*. New York: Routledge, 1994.

———. "Feminism Inside: Toward a Black Body Politic." In *Black Male*, edited by T. Golden. New York: Whitney Museum of American Art, 1995.

———. *We Real Cool. Black Men and Masculinity*. New York: Routledge, 2004.

Inda, Jonathan Xavier, and Renato Rosaldo, eds. *The Anthropology of Globalization: A Reader*. Malden: Blackwell Publishers, 2002.

Jackson, Bruce. *Get Your Ass in the Water and Swim Like Me*. Cambridge, Mass.: Harvard University Press, 1974.

Jafa, Arthur. "My Black Death." In *Everything but the Burden: What White People Are Taking from Black Culture*, edited by G. Tate, pp. 244–57. New York: Broadway Books, 2003.

Jefferson, Tony. "Muscle, 'Hard Men' and 'Iron' Mike Tyson: Reflections on Desire, Anxiety and the Embodiment of Masculinity." *Body & Society* 4, no. 1 (1998): 77–98.

Johnson, Charles. "The Phenomenology of the Black Body." *Michigan Quarterly Review* 32, no. 4 (1993): 598.

Johnson, E. Patrick. "Appropriating Blackness." In *Performance and the Politics of Authenticity*. Durham: Duke University Press, 2003.

Kaplan, E. Ann. "Rocking Around the Clock." In *Music Television, Postmodernism and Consumer Culture*. New York: Routledge, 1989.

Kelley, Robin D. G. "Race Rebels." In *Culture, Politics, and the Black Working Class*. New York: The Free Press, 1994.

Keyes, Cheryl L. *Rap Music and Street Consciousness*. Urbana: University of Illinois Press, 2002.

Kiesling, Scott F. "Dude." *American Speech* 79, no. 3 (2004): 281–305.

Langer, Susanne. *Philosophy in a New Key: A Study in the Symbolism of Reason, Rite and Art*. Cambridge, Mass.: Harvard University Press, 1942.

Lemelle, Anthony J. *Black Male Deviance*. Westport: Praeger, 1995.

Levitt, Steven D., and Stephen J. Dubner. *Freakonomics: A Rogue Economist Explores the Hidden Side of Everything*. New York: Penguin Books, 2005

Lewis, G. M. "The Distribution of the Negro in the Conterminous United States." *Geography* (November 1969): 411–16.

Lhamon, W. T. *Raising Cain. Blackface Performance from Jim Crow to Hip-hop*. Cambridge, Mass.: Harvard University Press, 1998.

Lipsitz, George. *Dangerous Crossroads. Popular Music, Postmodernism and the Poetics of Place*. London: Verso, 1994.

Lively, Adam. *Masks: Blackness, Race and the Imagination*. Oxford: Oxford University Press, 2000.

Lott, Eric. *Love and Theft. Blackface Minstrelsy and the American Working Class*. New York: Oxford University Press, 1995.

Mailer, Norman. *The White Negro: Superficial Reflections on the Hipster*. San Francisco: City Lights Books, 1969 [1957].

Majors, Richard, and Janet Mancini Billson. *Cool Pose. The Dilemmas of Black Manhood in America*. New York: Lexington Books, 1992.

Maultby, Portia. In *African American Music: An Introduction*, edited by Mellonee Burnim and Portia Maultsby. New York: Routledge, 2006.

McDonald, Paul. "Feeling and Fun. Romance, Dance and the Performing Male Body in the Take That Videos." In *Sexing the Groove. Popular Music and Gender*, edited by S. Whiteley. London: Routledge, 1997.

Menand, Louis. *American Studies*. New York: Farrar, Straus and Giroux, 2002.

Messerschmidt, James W. *Flesh & Blood. Adolescent Gender Diversity and Violence*. Lanham: Rowman & Littlefield, 2004.

Mezzrow, Mezz and Bernard Wolfe. *Really The Blues*. New York: Citadel Press, 1990 [1946].

Mitchell, Tony, ed. *Global Noise: Rap and Hip-Hop Outside the USA*. Middletown: Wesleyan University Press, 2001.

Monson, Ingrid. "The Problem with White Hipness: Race, Gender, and Cultural Conceptions in Jazz Historical Discourse." *Journal of the American Musicological Society* 48 (1995): 396–422.

Morrison, Toni. "Playing in the Dark." In *Whiteness and the Literary Imagination*. New York: Vintage Books, 1992.

Newitz, Annalee, and Matt Wray. "Introduction." In *White Trash. Race and Class in* America, edited by Annalee Newitz and Matt Wray. New York: Routledge, 1997.

Nixon, Sean. "Exhibiting Masculinity." In *Representation: Cultural Representations and Signifying Practices*, edited by S. Hall. London: Sage, 2003.

Norfleet, Dawn. "Hip-Hop and Rap." In *African American Music: An Introduction*, edited by Mellonee Burnim and Portia Maultsby. New York: Routledge, 2006.

Pollock, Sheldon. "The Cosmopolitan Vernacular." *Journal of Asian Studies* 57, no. 1 (1998): 6.

Radano, Ronald, and P. Bohlman, eds. *Music and the Racial Imagination*. Chicago: University of Chicago Press, 2000.

Roberts, John W. "From Trickster to Bad Man." In *The Black Folk Hero in Slavery and Freedom*. Philadelphia: University of Pennsylvania Press, 1989.

Roediger, David. "Guineas, Wiggers, and the Dramas of Racialized Culture." *American Literary History* 7, no. 4 (1995): 654–68.

Rony, Fatimah. *The Third Eye: Race, Cinema and Ethnographic Spectacle*. Durham: Duke University Press, 1996.

Root, Deborah. *Cannibal Culture: Art, Appropriation and the Commodification of Difference*. Boulder: Westview Press, 1998.

Rose, Anne E. "Documenting the American South: Thomas Nelson Page, 1853–1922" from the *Encyclopedia of Southern Culture*, edited by C. Wilson and W. Ferris, 1989. Retrieved July 1, 2009, from http://docsouth.unc.edu/southlit/pageolevir/bio.html.

Rose, Harold D. *The Black Ghetto. A Spatial Behavioral Perspective*. New York: McGraw-Hill, 1971.

Rose, Tricia. "Black Texts/Black Contexts." In *Black Popular Culture*, edited by G. Dent. Seattle: Bay Press, 1992.

———. *Black Noise. Rap Music and Black Culture in Contemporary America*. Middletown: Wesleyan University Press, 1994.

Ruby, Jay. *Picturing Culture. Explorations of Film & Anthropology*. Chicago: University of Chicago Press, 2000.

Rux, Carl Hancock. "Eminem: The New White Negro." In *Everything But The Burden: What White People Are Taking From Black Culture*, edited by G. Tate, ed. New York: Broadway Books, 2003.

Samuels, David. "The Rap on Rap: The 'Black Music' That Isn't Either." In *Rap On Rap: Straight-Up Talk on Hip-hop* Culture, edited by A. Sexton. New York: Delta, 1995.

Schloss, Joseph. *Foundation: B-Boys, B-Girls, and Hip-hop Culture in New York*. New York: Oxford University Press, 2009.

Schou, Nick. *Kill the Messenger: How the CIA's Crack-Cocaine Controversy Destroyed Journalist Gary Webb*. New York: National Books, 2006.

Seabrook, John. *Nobrow: The Culture of Marketing, the Marketing of Culture*. New York: Vintage Books, 2000.

Shanahan, Dan. *Language, Feeling, and the Brain: The Evocative Vector*. New Brunswick: Transaction Publishers, 2007.

———. "A New View of Language, Emotion and the Brain." *Integrative Psychological & Behavioral Science* 42, no. 1 (2008).

Small, Christopher. *Music of the Common Tongue: Survival and Celebration in African American Music*. Middletown: Wesleyan University Press, 1987.

———. "Africans, Europeans and the Making of Music." In *Signifyin(g), Sanctifying' & Slam Dunking. A Reader in African American Expressive Culture*, edited by Gena Dagel Caponi. Amherst: University of Massachusetts Press, 1999.

Stallybrass, Peter, and Allen White. *The Politics and Poetics of Transgression*. London: Methuen, 1986.

Stock, Brian. *The Implications of Literacy: Written Language and Models of Interpretation in the Eleventh and Twelfth Centuries*. Princeton: Princeton University Press, 1983.

Stout, Gene. "Gangsta Bad Boy. Getting His Two Cents In. 50 Cent's Dangerous Life Pervades His Rap." *Seattle Post-Intelligencer*, May 9, 2003, 3.

Sweeney, Gael. "The King of White Trash Culture. Elvis Presley and the Aesthetics of Excess." In *White Trash. Race and Class in America*, edited by M.a.A.N. Wray. New York: Routledge, 1997.

Szatmary, David P. *A Time To Rock. A Social History of Rock and Roll*. New York: Schirmer Books, 1996.

Tamene, Getnet. "Political Ethics and the Human Polity: The African Dimension." In *Economic and Political Development Ethics: Europe and Beyond*, edited by Bruno S. Sergi and William T. Bagatelas, 123. Bratislava: Iura Edition, Bratislava, 2007.

Tucker, Linda. *Lockstep and Dance. Images of Black Men in Popular Culture*. Jackson: University of Mississippi Press, 2007.

Tucker, Sherrie. "Issues of Gender: Jazz. ." In *African American Music: An Introduction*, edited by Mellonee Burnim and Portia Maultsby. New York: Routledge, 2006.

Van Vechten, Carl. *Nigger Heaven*. Urbana: University of Illinois Press, 2000 [1926].

Walser, Robert. *Running With The Devil. Power, Gender, and Madness in Heavy Metal Music*. Hanover: Wesleyan University Press, 1993.

Ware, Vron, and Les Back. *Out of Whiteness. Color, Politics and Culture*. Chicago: University of Chicago Press, 2002.

Webb, Gary. *Dark Alliance: The CIA, the Contras, and the Crack Cocaine Explosion*. New York: Seven Stories Press, 2003 [1998].

Wepman, Dennis, Ronald Newman, and Murray Binderman. *The Life. The Lore and Folk Poetry of the Black Hustler*. Pittsburgh: University of Pittsburgh Press, 1976.

West, Cornel. *Race Matters*. New York: Vintage Books, 1994.

———. *Democracy Matters. Winning the Fight Against Imperialism*. New York: Penguin Press, 2004.

White, Miles. "The Phonograph Turntable and Performance Practice in Hip Hop Music." *Ethnomusicology Online*. Vol. 2. 1996. Retrieved at http://www.umbc.edu/eol/2/white.

White, Shane, and Graham White. *Stylin': African American Expressive Culture from Its Beginnings to the Zoot Suit*. Ithaca: Cornell University Press, 1998.

———. "Strolling, Jooking, and Fixy Clothes." In *Signifyin(g), Sanctifyin' & SlamDunking*, edited by G. D. Caponi, 434. Amherst: University of Massachusetts, 1999.

Whitehead, Stephen M. *Men and Masculinities. Key Themes and New Directions*. Malden, Mass.: Blackwell (USA), 2002.

Whiteley, Sheila. "Little Red Rooster v. The Honky Tonk Woman. Mick Jagger, Sexuality, Style and Image." In *Sexing the Groove. Popular Music and Gender*, edited by S. Whiteley. London: Routledge, 1997.

Williams, Robert F. *Negroes With Guns*. Detroit: Wayne State University, 1998 [1962].

Wilson, William Julius. *The Truly Disadvantaged: The Inner City, the Underclass, and Public Policy*. Chicago: University of Chicago Press, 1990.

———, ed. *The Ghetto Underclass: Social Science Perspectives*. Newbury Park: Sage, 1993.

Wilson-Brown, Carrie, and Cameron McCarthy. "The Organization of Affect: Popular Music, Youth, and Intellectual and Political Life (An Interview with Larry Grossberg)." In *Sound Identities: Popular Music and the Cultural Politics of Education*, edited by C. McCarthy, G. Hudak, S. Miklaucic, and P. Saukko. New York: Peter Lang, 1999.

Wilson, Olly. "The Heterogeneous Sound Ideal in African-American Music." In *Signifyin(g), Sanctifying' & Slam Dunking. A Reader in African American Expressive Culture*, edited by Gena Dagel Caponi. Amherst: University of Massachusetts Press, 1999.

Wise, Mike. "Opinions on the NBA's Dress Code Are Far From Uniform." *The Washington Post*. Retrieved on July 2, 2009, from http://www.washingtonpost.com/wp-dyn/content/article/2005/10/22/AR2005102201386.html.

Wong, Deborah. "The Asian American Body in Performance." In *Music and the Racial Imagination*, edited by R.a.P.B. Radano, 57–94. Chicago: University of Chicago Press, 2000.

Wynter, Leon E. *American Skin: Pop Culture, Big Business and the End of White America*. New York: Crown Publishers, 2002.

# Index

*absent black presence*, 6, 7, 99, 111; male deviant and, 107

*affecting (black) presence*, 83, 89

affecting media, 35, 36, 135

affective gestures, 18, 106

affective strategies, 18, 23, 98

African American music, 1, 47, 56, 89, 141n38

African/black American culture, 18, 27, 29–30, 129, 137n2; becoming more educated, 56; hip-hop culture and, 131; Japanese youth and, 29; reduced to negative, 3; as a source of education, 94; as a source of performing style, 26; understanding/recognition of, 30. *See also* black culture

African/black Americans, 10, 14, 45, 119, 128; hurt by crack cocaine, 78; imaginings of, 131; middle-class, 69, 73; minstrelsy and, 11; Otherization of, 146n49; as outsiders, 25, 65, 90; political activism of, 119; urban, 98; visual/grotesque representations of, 10, 14, 27, 29. *See also* blacks

Afrika Bambaataa, 35, 48; "Looking for the Perfect Beat," 48; "Planet Rock," 48, 49; *Renegades of Funk,* 48

albinism: and Brother Ali, 116, 118–19

Alger, Horatio, 81, 85

Ali, Muhammad, 66–67, 81, 85

American culture, 1, 4, 6, 14, 16, 18

American Dream, 47, 80, 81, 118

American popular music, 1, 24, 64, 85; *absent black presence* in, 6; *black brute cum street thug* in, 69; mainstream, 49, 75

Anderson, Victor, 108, 146n34

appropriation, 92–96; affective, 93; of black expressive tropes, 106; of blackness/black body/subjectivity, 15, 22, 90, 112, 120, 124; cross-/black cultural, 27, 90, 92; white, 20, 104

Armstrong, Louis, 17, 51, 95

authenticity, 38–39, 70–71, 86–87, 92–93, 103–8; aggressive behavior and, 26; of Beastie Boys, 99, 101; black, 28; of black performers of minstrelsy, 13; contestations around, 6; of Elvis, 92; of Eminem, 112; increased demands for, 97; of Jay-Z, 83; in *Les Negres,* 73, 86; powerful masculine, 64; requirements of new, 115; street dances and, 42; urban space and, 39; of Vanilla Ice, 103; of vernacular language, 57

Ayler, Albert, 17

bad man: African American male as, 133; Ali, Muhammad as, 66; Brother Ali as, 117, 124; Eminem and, 114; hardcore rappers as, 72, 74, 112; Jay-Z as, 81, 85, 86; Mike Tyson as, 68; vs. bad nigger, 64–65

bad nigger, 3–4, 64–69, 71–72; Beastie Boys as, 98; blacks as potential, 69; Brother Ali as not, 117, 124; Eminem as, 114; 50 Cent as, 129; ghetto narratives involving, 87; hardcore gangsta figure as, 28; Ice Cube as, 72; Jack Johnson as, 67; Jay-Z as, 81, 82, 84, 85; N.W.A as, 64, 75; Obama's counterpoint to, 133; as troublemaker, 65; Mike

Formerly a professional musician and entertainment journalist, **MILES WHITE** teaches at City University of Seattle in Slovakia.

## AFRICAN AMERICAN MUSIC IN GLOBAL PERSPECTIVE

Black Women and Music: More than the Blues
  *Edited by Eileen M. Hayes and Linda F. Williams*
Ramblin' on My Mind: New Perspectives on the Blues
  *Edited by David Evans*
Follow Your Heart: Moving with the Giants of Jazz, Swing, and Rhythm and Blues
  *Joe Evans with Christopher Brooks*
Songs in Black and Lavender: Race, Sexual Politics, and Women's Music
  *Eileen M. Hayes*
From Jim Crow to Jay-Z: Race, Rap, and the Performance of Masculinity
  *Miles White*

The University of Illinois Press
is a founding member of the
Association of American University Presses.

---

Composed in 10.5/13 Adobe Minion Pro
with Futura Heavy display
at the University of Illinois Press
Manufactured by Thomson-Shore, Inc.

University of Illinois Press
1325 South Oak Street
Champaign, IL 61820-6903
www.press.uillinois.edu